THE
JESUS
REPORT

THE
JESUS
REPORT

JOHANNES LEHMANN

TRANSLATED BY MICHAEL HERON

SOUVENIR PRESS/Publishers/London

First published in the United States 1971
by Stein and Day/New York
First British Edition 1972 by Souvenir Press Ltd,
95 Mortimer Street, London W.1, and simultaneously
in Canada by J. M. Dent & Sons (Canada) Ltd, Ontario, Canada

English Translation Copyright © 1971 by Souvenir Press
Copyright © 1970 under title
Jesus-Report: Protokoll einer Verfalschung by Econ Verlag GmbH

ISBN 0 285 62022 3

Printed in Great Britain by
Fletcher & Son Ltd, Norwich

CONTENTS

ALL institutions have an innate tendency to settle down and become complacent, and try hard to show that they have a value per se. The institution of the church has not escaped this ideological process, either, and so it has needed control and revision just like other organizations. It is neither sacrosanct nor untouchable, and it has frequently had to accept reinterpretations during the two thousand years of its existence, whether it wanted to or not.

All these reinterpretations were based on the assumption that with the passage of time the institution of the church had moved too far away from its original program, because unlike other religions Christianity claims to have a historical origin and to be based on a historical personage who lived in a historical and consequently verifiable age.

So if new facts are discovered that explain the accepted historical background better or differently, the church has to orient its teaching and its "message" toward what was originally meant, and not toward what has grown out of it in the course of two thousand years. Yet for nearly two thousand years we did not know of a single document from those days, apart from the actual Bible, that could have confirmed, cast doubt on, or amended the life and teaching of Jesus of Nazareth.

But owing to one of those incalculable accidents of history, we have now had for twenty years a series of documents that throw an entirely new light on the historical background of the Christian faith. We find ideas, words, and whole sentences from the New Testament in them, although they were written before the birth of Jesus of Nazareth. They are the famous Dead Sea scrolls, which were found in 1947 and are the ancient scriptures of a Jewish monastic sect, the Essenes, who lived around the birth of Christ in Qumran, a settlement on the Dead Sea.

Is it possible that Jesus was not the creator of a new personal doctrine? Did he only repeat what others had thought before him? Then who was the real founder of Christianity? Was he really the "Christ" from whom Christians take their name?

The churches cling firmly to this belief, even though they admit that today Jesus of Nazareth would not agree with everything that has happened since he died. Yet in spite of their admitted inflexibility, they claim to teach basically what Jesus taught.

Since the discovery of the Dead Sea scrolls we are entitled to doubt even this, but in spite of the immense amount of specialized literature that has been written about the scrolls, the churches remain silent. They state their position on many subjects, but they are allergic when it comes to the question of the historical truth and hence of their own axiomatic existence. They admit, because they are forced to, the astonishing similarity between the original Christian church and its doctrine, and the Dead Sea scrolls, but believe they can disprove the resemblance because the sources do not tally exactly. This runs counter to experience, and the critic notices the lack of sound scholarly methodology. The New Testament, too, is full of contradictions—for all the frequently emphasized uniformity of its aims.

The reason for this is historical development. For a long time theologians have known that the New Testament scriptures we use are not preserved in their original version. It is demonstrable that the further away they were in time from the death of Jesus of Nazareth, the more the different authors of the gospels deviated from the original. Paul, who never saw Jesus and carried the "gospel" from the cramped Jewish world to the Greek sphere of culture and so inevitably distorted it, was long ago called the first falsifier of Christianity. But it was not clear how far Christianity had departed from its original aims even in the first century A.D. until the discovery of the Dead Sea scrolls.

The church finds it hard to defend itself against its members' inability to believe, and the number of people who feel this conflict more or less consciously is growing. Today these marginal members, whose only connection with the church is often the celebration of family events, such as weddings and christenings, are readier than ever to pose and discuss the question of the real Jesus and the present-day church.

This book assembles the facts necessary for this discussion. Fundamentally what it supplies is not so much new as unfamiliar information, because in the past scholars and theologians did not always pass on their knowledge to members of the church, or at least not impartially. It is an attempt to free the knowledge of experts from ideological and emotive accretions, and present it lucidly and intelligently. That is one reason—though not the only one—why I give the man from Nazareth, to whom each one of us adopts a positive or negative attitude, the neutral designation of "Rabbi J."

"What is truth?" asked Pontius Pilate nearly two thousand years ago. The question is still valid today, and it is a question the church has to ask itself today as it did in the past.

For perhaps church and Christianity are no longer identical and we simply do not see it. Perhaps faith has been replaced by ideology and we do not perceive it. Perhaps Rabbi J. would not be a member of a "Christian church" today and we dare not face the possibility. Perhaps we are equating things that are not really connected, because the blind spot in our eyes deceives us. Perhaps everything is quite different from what is currently accepted. That at least is the theme of the "mystery of Rabbi J." that can be discussed and written about today on the basis of the sources available to us.

One

THE BLIND SPOT

Nᴏɴᴇ of us ever knew Rabbi J. Everything that we have been able to learn about him and his extraordinary life, we know through intermediaries, for Rabbi J. is dead. And even the intermediaries did not know him. Theirs were not eyewitness accounts, and for some time people believed that that might be the reason for the confusion and the strange obscurity surrounding Rabbi J.'s life. For the more they depended on the different and frequently contradictory accounts, the further Rabbi J. retreated.

To many people Rabbi J. was like a star in the sky that becomes invisible at the very moment that we look at it directly, yet twinkles again when we look past it, because a remarkable caprice of nature has arranged the blind spot in our eyes so that anything we gaze at intently remains in darkness.

In other words, if we begin to look past Rabbi J., and his face no longer holds the center of the stage, we learn more about him. The less we look at him, the better we can get to know him; the hazier the Rabbi's face, the clearer his life.

In his views, wishes, and dreams, he differs ever more sharply from the figure propagated by his biographers and created by his worshipers.

As we soon notice, neither group told the story of

Rabbi J.; they simply mirrored their own destinies in his life. They said Rabbi J., but they meant themselves; they projected their difficulties on to him and transferred their hopes to him. They made a legend out of Rabbi J., because they did not, could not—and did not want to—understand him.

For example, Rabbi J. was a Jew—the title "Rabbi" makes that clear to everyone—but hardly anyone who knows anything about him faces up to the fact; reluctantly people feel that he may have looked like the man next door, only rather more distinguished. Legends adapt themselves, especially when it is not considered to be an advantage to be a Jew. We know no picture that shows him as an Israelite, with a dark skin and large, hooked nose, and wearing a burnoose, as was usual in his day when the region was still called Palestine. Rabbi J. has even lost his face, although there is a description of him. The Roman official Lentulus describes him as having "nut-brown hair, that is smooth down to the ears and from the ears downward forms soft curls and flows on to his shoulders in luxuriant locks, with a parting in the center of his head after the fashion of the Nazarenes, a smooth clear brow, and a reddish face without spots or wrinkles. Nose and mouth are flawless, he wears a full luxuriant beard, which is the same color as his hair and is parted in the middle; he has blue-gray eyes with an unusually varied capacity for expression. . . ."[1]

Today we still see these figures with beards like Moses, venerable patriarchs in caftans, by the Wailing Wall in Jerusalem; we meet the same types with brown earlocks as they stand by Abraham's tomb at Hebron, muttering prayers and swaying constantly like pendulums. And why should Rabbi J. have looked any different from his descendants?

Historians doubt if this description is genuine, for why should a Roman have described a Jew so generously? Everyone knows what Jews look like. But why did Lentulus say that "he was of medium height, fifteen and a half fists tall"?[2] Who would bother to invent a detail like that, for a height of just under five feet was nothing special even in those days, and who would contradict all the other accounts by saying: "...he is cheerful in seriousness; sometimes he weeps, but no one has ever seen him laugh"?[3]

Who was this Rabbi J.? One thing is clear: he was a Palestinian Jew and probably he did not wash as often as we consider necessary nowadays.

He spoke Aramaic, a language that is no longer spoken today; he lived in a barren wilderness, in which a modest plantation around a spring is still called *pardesh* after the ancient word for paradise; he lived in a world in which water was so precious that at baptism it was made the symbol of the conversion from life hitherto to real life; in the solitude of an interminable landscape he saw the glittering stars of a hot desert night; he prayed to an invisible God who was never portrayed and whose name Jews hold too sacred to pronounce even today; he lived in different scenery and in a different world from ours, and the things he took for granted are foreign to us. And if you have not been in the Judaean desert and near the Dead Sea, if you do not speak his language and do not live in the same tradition and world of ideas—and only a Jew can do so —then you will never really understand Rabbi J.

So my attempt to write about his life is difficult. I am not a Jew and I grew up in the Christian West. I start off with the best premises for misunderstanding him, even though I know all about the Pharisees and Sadducees, the Temple at Jerusalem, the Babylonian exile, and the major and minor prophets. For in my opinion nearly everyone in the Christian West who has studied or written about the Jew J. has inevitably misinterpreted or misunderstood him.

The reason for this is that Rabbi J.'s life has passed through two filters. One filter made people obscure his life from the very beginning for their own special reasons, because they dared not put down the true motives behind it. So some of the difficulties are obviously in the life of the man himself. His actual life is in opposition to his biography, and only the fact that the obfuscation was not wholly successful enables us to discover the true motives, by doing a little detective work and thinking logically, and so draw a new picture of him.

The second filter did not so much obscure as distort his life. Its effect was to make the already vague picture lose nearly all its individual features. The Rabbi became his own legend simply because after a certain time people no longer understood or wanted to understand many details of his life and so arrived at a new personal interpretation against which he could no longer defend himself.

There is an amazingly simple example in Rabbi J.'s life of how translators could misunderstand the elementary meaning of words by trying to be too profound, just because they were not Jews. One of the stories about Rabbi J. begins by mentioning a day without telling us to what it refers. The passage reads: "And the third day there was a marriage in Cana of Galilee; and the mother of J. was there: And both J. was called, and his disciples, to the marriage."[4]

Nowhere in the gospel according to St. John do we hear about the first or second day, although the previous more or less connected stories are introduced on three occasions by the locution "the next day." Whichever way one reckons the "third day" is either unintelligible or unnecessary. For this reason many translators have had trouble with this passage. One of them left the apparently unintelligible words out and wrote: "There was a marriage at Cana in Galilee."

A modern German translation reads: "Three days later a marriage feast took place at Cana, a town in Galilee."[5] While another modern translation, which says, "Two days later a marriage took place at Cana in Galilee,"[6] is talking absolute nonsense, for if Rabbi J. was still by the Dead Sea, he would have had to cover the seventy-five miles from Jericho to Cana in one day to be at the wedding the day after next.

Many theologians interpreted the "third" day symbolically. Because turning the water into wine at the marriage in Cana was Rabbi J.'s first miracle, they saw in this a secret reference to the Resurrection, the miraculous event which also took place on a third day. Thus the marriage at Cana prefigured the image of the "heavenly bridegroom."

In any case the passage is obscure, if not completely unintelligible, to a Christian; it is not to a Jew. He can translate the Greek of the New Testament back into Hebrew and see what the Aramaic original might really have meant. For all the information about Rabbi J. has come down to us in a foreign language, namely Greek. The Jewish religious scholar Shalom Ben Chorin writes about this passage in his book *J.—the Nazarene from the Jewish Point of View:* "But if we translate the text back into Hebrew, into the atmosphere and background to which it belongs, we read: *U bayom hashlishi.* . . . *Yom hashlishi*, the third day, is simply Tuesday, because the Jewish week begins on Sunday and ends on the seventh day, the Sabbath. The individual days have no names, with the exception of the Sabbath or Shabbath, which means day of rest. They are only numbered first, second, third day, etc., and the third day, Tuesday, was and still is the classical day for Jewish marriages, for it is *Kephel ki tov*, the day of the twice-repeated "it was good" in the story of the creation in Genesis (1:10, 12).

Although the Talmud prescribes Wednesday as the day for the marriage of virgins, Tuesday, the third, was then and still is preferred as a wedding day by simple country folk—and those are the kind of people we are talking about in Galilee.

Twice in the Bible it says "for it was good," so that one *ki tov* applies to the bridegroom and another to the bride, and they will enjoy a doubly fortunate marriage.

That is the simple solution of the puzzling time reference in the story of the marriage at Cana. Scholars have made a tremendous mystery out of this third day, but none of them realized that it was no more than a Jewish farmers' wedding in Galilee.

For nearly two thousand years scholars laboriously probed mysteries that were no mysteries, and we may well ask why no Old Testament scholar ever drew the attention of his fellow experts on the New Testament to the Jewish system of numbering the days of the week. A New Testament scholar might even have noticed it on his own if he had visited the museum on the Acropolis in Athens. The museum is closed on Tuesdays and a notice in Greek says merely: "Closed on the third day," for the Greeks still number the days of the week like the Jews, as they did in the past.

So there are still a whole series of ideas in the stories about Rabbi J. that become more nonsensical the more exactly and literally they are rendered, because no one bothers to ask what they meant in their original cultural context. We shall see that the mere fact of translating ideas into another linguistic and mental world can cause radical misapprehensions that completely distort and falsify the actual teaching of Rabbi J. and his own assessment of himself. The unnecessary mystification about an ordinary day of the week is the most harmless example. There are cases where translators, rendering the original literally and so making nonsense of it, have brought into being whole dogmas by reading into the misunderstood passages new religious concepts from their own culture and thus contradicting the original aims of Rabbi J.'s teaching.

But to begin with I should like to stick to the historical sequence of events and talk about the first filter that obscured and made a mystery of Rabbi J.'s life from the very beginning.

At first sight it looks as if Rabbi J. had the misfortune to choose followers who were rather simpleminded. Every time he tells a parable, the disciples say that they do not understand it and ask what it means. This could be a stylistic trick of the evangelists to give Rabbi J. a chance to explain, but the disciples were not really stupid. Obviously the parables were deliberately formulated so that they could not be understood straightforwardly. Obviously they contained, besides the literal meaning of the words, a second, hidden, meaning which only initiates understood. A passage in the New Testament makes that clear: "And the disciples came, and said unto him, Why speakest thou unto them in parables? He answered and said unto them, Because it is given unto you to know the mysteries of the kingdom of heaven, but to them it is not given. For whosoever hath, to him shall be given, and he shall have more abundance: but whosoever hath not, from him shall be taken away even that he hath. Therefore speak I to them in parables: because they seeing see not; and hearing they hear not, neither do they understand.... But blessed are your eyes, for they see: and your ears, for they hear."[8]

The essence of the parables is over and over again the coming of the kingdom of heaven, the secret of the kingdom, the kingdom of God, and as the New Testament says: "Hear ye therefore the parable of the sower. When any one heareth the word of the kingdom [of God], and understandeth it not. . . ."[9]

There was really nothing to understand. Expectation of the end of the world or at least the end of the Roman occupation and a kingdom set up by God was common ideological currency at the time. What Rabbi J. said was quite in keeping with Mosaic Jewish thought; John the Baptist had preached the very same thing and the Old Testament is full of such expectations. So where was the secret? Why could not everyone know and understand what he said? The idea suggests itself that the Rabbi's words concealed another secret that was not explicit, that they had a double meaning as in a mystery religion. His audience obviously felt this, too: "And it came to pass, when Jesus had ended these sayings, the people were astonished at his doctrine: For he taught them as one having authority, and not as the scribes."[10]

But what was the other thing he taught? Because it is the best conclusion we can draw from the gospel stories, we have grown accustomed to talking about the doctrine of love as opposed to that of the law. Yet if that was the essence of his teaching, what was there to make a mystery about? Anyone who thumbs through the Talmud keeps on coming across ideas about love and loving one's neighbor. It must have been something else that was accessible only to initiates and had to be guarded like the secret of the Messiah. A secret that only men whom God had given the necessary insight understood. As it says at the end of many parables that J. told the people without explanation: "He that hath ears to hear, let him hear."

What was there to hear? I claim that this is the blind spot that results from looking straight at the figure of Rabbi J. So I am trying to look past him to his environment, his age, and his fellow men. For I do not want to tell the story of Rabbi J. in the way that Europeans have done for nearly two thousand years. I want to discover the Rabbi J. whom his contemporaries knew, honored, or despised.

In spite of the tremendous impact the life and ideas of Rabbi J. have made on the world—his birth is still the caesura on which we base our chronology—there is not a single contemporary description of his life. Not even the Jewish historian Flavius Josephus, who wrote a detailed history of the Jewish people in the first century A.D., knew him. The only sentence in Josephus, "J., who was called the Messiah, is worshiped by a community in Jerusalem,"[1] is not by him, but is a later addition, and the Roman historian Tacitus, who is the only profane source to mention the Jew J., merely writes in explanation of the name "Christiani": "Christus, from whom their name comes, was condemned to death by the Procurator Pontius Pilate in the reign of the Emperor Tiberius."[2]

Rabbi J. himself has not left a single line behind. So what we know about him is based solely on the three sources of information which are contained in the New Testament. One source is the epistles of St. Paul, who never saw or heard Rabbi J. The second consists of a no longer extant original text from which later came the three so-called synoptic—i.e., comparable—gospels of Matthew, Mark, and Luke, and the third is the gospel according to St. John, which is based on a quite different tradition.

All four gospels appeared more than a generation after Rabbi J.'s death and were written and edited by people who were demonstrably not eyewitnesses, but secondhand reporters.

As we know, the four accounts frequently contradict each other. That may be because each of the "eyewitnesses" saw, heard, or remembered what happened in a different way, but it may also be because the definitive editors brought the accounts up to date by their contemporary standards and "improved" them. For example, Rabbi J. could not possibly have spoken his last words in the three different versions found in the New Testament. Unless we assume that he spoke all three versions one after the other while he was on the cross and each evangelist only reported one (why, one wonders), the only remaining possibility is that at least two of J.'s utterances were invented.

Mark, the earliest gospel, ends J.'s life with the cry of despair: "My God, my God, why hast thou forsaken me?" We find this in Matthew, too, the next account in time. In Luke, who already gives a detailed description of the spread of Christianity in his Acts of the Apostles, the idealization of Christ's death, at a greater distance from the historical event, is already reflected. (The recently formed church interpreted J.'s death similarly in retrospect.) The last words Luke gives are "Father, into thy hands I commend my spirit." Here despair and the life crowned with failure have already become acceptance. And in John, the gospel that was written last, we find triumph and victory: "It is finished." A plan had been put into effect. There is no trace of failure and the terror of the disciples who ran away after his death, because inconvenient truths ought not to exist. A veil was cast over the painful memory; the truth was corrected.

If we work from the premise that a certain fact in Rabbi J.'s life was not stated and could not be made public, there is yet a third explanation of how the contradictions in the gospels arose: all those passages that touched on the secret or whose wording suggested associations with it to the readers of those days had to be made unrecognizable. This could be done by omission, adaptation, or additional explanations. As each of the evangelists set about the task differently, the result of their labors was the contradictory accounts we have today.

For example, when the Roman soldiers came to arrest Rabbi J. "with swords and staves," and the aggressive Peter promptly chopped off Malchus's ear, we accept it as a bit of convincing realism. But how did Peter, the disciple, get hold of a sword in the first place? And how is it possible that the very man who preached love and atonement, also said: "Think not that I am come to send peace on earth: I came not to send peace, but a sword."[3]

How was it that a man who let himself be called Messiah and savior forbade his disciples to tell others about it? How could a man who merely summoned people to lead a God-fearing life clash with the Roman occupation forces, who executed him as a political criminal; and who can explain why the first Christians in Jerusalem, who felt themselves to be devout Jews and prayed every day in the temple without any intention of starting a schism, were nevertheless persecuted by Paul as if they were conspirators?

There is something inconsistent here. Rabbi J.'s picture is drawn so that it has two facets. Consequently scholars have often tried to oppose to the naïve harmless image of a wandering preacher that the majority make out of Rabbi J. the revolutionary and agitator J., because they suspected the real reason for all the mystery there.

Lastly, Joel Carmichael, in his book *The Death of J.*, has tried to show that Rabbi J. was nothing but a political rebel against the Roman occupation forces. At first Rabbi J. attempted an uprising by peaceful means, but then became convinced that nothing could be accomplished without the sword. That is how we should understand the isolated passage in Luke where J. asks: "When I sent you without purse, and scrip, and shoes, lacked ye any thing? And they said, Nothing. Then said he unto them, But now, he that hath a purse, let him take it, and likewise his scrip; and he that hath no sword, let him sell his garment, and buy one."[5]

According to Carmichael, he entered Jerusalem with a small armed force and was hailed as the Messiah, the people's liberator. What the evangelist toned down into the purging of the temple was really the occupation of the temple by J., the rebel — surely an exaggeration. Afterward he had to flee and spend the night outside the walls of Jerusalem.

At all events it is true that at some point in time close to his entry into Jerusalem and the purging of the temple, Rabbi J. was in hiding outside the city walls (otherwise Judas would not have had to betray the hiding place), and that he was executed by the Romans on the political charge that he called himself the King of the Jews. Carmichael sums it up as follows: "In our own terms, Jesus was a national leader, one of the many who as we have seen sprang up among the Jews during their long-drawn-out subjugation by Rome."[6]

Failure would also explain the cry of despair: "My God, my God, why hast thou forsaken me?" Later the evangelists saw to it that this portrait was "piously retouched to smooth away those aspects of Jesus' enterprise that were to prove indigestible to later Christian theory—the violence that attended Jesus' movement, its anti-Roman political implications, and above all, perhaps, its material failure—all were either forgotten or obliterated in the new perspective of Jesus' cultic magnification."[7]

This thesis of Carmichael's is attractive insofar as it gives a factual explanation of how such an apparently harmless, devout man came into conflict with the occupying power and was treated on the same level as Barabbas, an agitator.

If the Jew J. was judged by the Romans—and he was —then it must have been for a political crime. That is the only possible interpretation. But now we can understand why the evangelists draw a onesidedly devout picture of Rabbi J. and conceal the political aspects of his life as far as possible. If the Rabbi's steadily increasing following was to exist in the Roman Empire's sphere of influence, the authors of the New Testament must have felt obliged to play down any opposition to the occupying government.

According to Carmichael, therein lies the real mystery of the man J., which he legitimately links up with the concept of the Messiah, whom the Jews looked on as a national liberator at God's behest. When liberation by this Messiah failed, the later Christians—according to Carmichael—introduced the suffering Messiah, for whom there is no prototype in Jewish history. In other words they completely transformed the proper functions of the Messiah.

Carmichael's theory certainly clears up a political aspect of Rabbi J.'s life which undoubtedly existed but which is not immediately recognizable after the retouching of two thousand years. In my opinion, however, this explanation does not reveal the whole of Rabbi J.'s secret, but only the part that led to his death.

What Carmichael leaves out for convenience' sake are all those passages where Rabbi J. is attacked for his ethical and religious teaching. A hostility to the scribes and Pharisees that is never explained or justified runs right through the gospels. We have grown accustomed —somewhat unjustly—to looking on the Pharisees as formalists and hypocrites, whose dead faith in the Mosaic law was opposed to the message of Rabbi J., whom we see as a reformer to whom what truly mattered was the real law of God. But why on earth should anyone think that this "fool from Galilee" was such a dangerous opponent that desperate measures had to be taken to get rid of him? If he preached a new doctrine at which the people marveled, it would hardly have consisted of the announcement that he was planning a revolt and consequently was some kind of Messiah, a liberator from servitude. Anyone who has read a smattering of the Jewish history of that period knows that it literally teemed with rebels and revolts. In other words the new teaching must have had a different emphasis—an emphasis that also justified the conflict with the Pharisees.

For about two hundred years before and after the birth of Christ, the Pharisees and Sadducees were the two great dominant currents in Jewish life. They differed mainly in their attitude to the Torah, the collection of Jewish laws. Carmichael writes on the subject:

"Ever since Ezra (444 b.c.) the Torah had been the unchallenged religious source of religious authority for the whole of the Jewish people. Since it had been fixed in writing, however, it was obviously incapable of dealing with every specific problem that might arise in the course of time.

"The Sadducees, as the aristocratic, priestly group, held the view that the Torah as written had to be supplemented by priestly decisions as the occasion arose. Thus the scope of the Torah tended to contract gradually with time.

"The Pharisees, on the other hand, believed that the Torah was binding not merely by virtue of the collective oath taken by the representatives of the people in the time of Ezra but also because it was the direct expression of God's will. They enlarged the scope of the Torah, and made this socially feasible by evolving the concept of an Oral Law. This was as ancient as the words of the written Torah itself, and just as binding."[8]

The Sadducees were conservative, whereas the Pharisees—the product of what we would call today a "pietistic" movement of *Chasidim*, or devout—acquired a reputation for hypocrisy because they always had an explanation ready for every situation, even when it was not covered by the Torah. But it is possible to take a different view of them, as Carmichael does: "The Sadducees were conservative guardians of an ancient text; they considered the Pharisees innovators who acted as disturbers of the public order and as gadflies generally. . . . In the time of J. the Pharisees, without being political, were essentially oppositionists; they found many sympathizers among those irked by the rule of the Sadducees."

The question is why our Rabbi, who had publicly proclaimed the kind of innovations that forced people to attack him, attacked the Pharisees and not the Sadducees. For it was really the Pharisees with their flexibility and adaptability who should have been less scandalized by Rabbi J. than the orthodox Sadducees. If Rabbi J. was an innovator, he should have found sympathy among the Pharisees rather than the Sadducees, especially as the Sadducees were closely connected with the government and the temple, and for that very reason would inevitably have taken offense at any revolutionary deviation from their religious and political point of view.

The New Testament paints a different picture. There

Rabbi J. is always clashing with the Pharisees, but he comes into conflict with the Sadducees only when resurrection and expectation of the end of the world are concerned. For the Sadducees did not believe in resurrection and had no sympathy with apocalyptic ideas of the kind traditionally ascribed to Rabbi J.

Now we see Rabbi J. more clearly—a man with everyone's hand against him who preached the joyful message of the coming of God's kingdom and was driven to his death as an unwelcome individualist because the religious establishment had the power and so had right on its side.

But was Rabbi J. a solitary prophet? According to the New Testament it looks as if he was. In it there are only two movements: the Pharisees and Sadducees. Rabbi J. (and John the Baptist, too) differed from both of them. But now we know from a profane nonbiblical source that there was a third religious group in existence at the time. There is not a single word about it in the New Testament, either for or against, although it too was a product of the movement of the Chasidim and so originally related to the Pharisees.

It was a religious movement, numerically about as strong as the Pharisees, which expected the imminent end of the world and preached repentance and reformation because the kingdom of God was at hand. This third group, whose renewal of faith made them adhere to the law all the more strictly because they thought that the priests in the Temple at Jerusalem were corrupt, had one distinguishing feature that was unknown in the whole history of the Jewish faith before: they were monks. Western history has accustomed us to the idea that monks are part and parcel of the religious life. But even what we accept as axiomatic was once revolutionary. We have only to read about the effect that John the Baptist, a hermit in a camel's-hair cloak, had on the people of Jerusalem: they made a pilgrimage to him in the desert and were baptized, and among them was Rabbi J.

This third religious reformist movement, which Rabbi J. neither mentions nor attacks, was, unlike the Pharisees and Sadducees, a secret cult inside Judaism. Strict rules, which included starvation as a punishment for the monks, forbade the revelation of the secrets of the inner circle, access to which was possible only after a waiting period and initiation rites.

Now if we assume that Rabbi J. was close to this sect or even belonged to it, would not the fact that he appeared in public and yet had sworn to keep the mysteries secret explain those passages which we find obscure, unintelligible, or contradictory, because they do not express clearly what it was forbidden to express?

Is this Rabbi J.'s secret? That as a strict orthodox Jew, expecting the imminent arrival of the kingdom of God like John the Baptist, he preached a doctrine which was only for initiates and which he dared utter only in ambiguous parables? He who hath ears to hear, let him hear.

Unlike the authors of the New Testament, Flavius Josephus, the Jewish historian, wastes very few words on the Pharisees and Sadducees, but nineteen hundred years ago he described in astonishing detail the secret sect which he expressly calls the third force in the Jewish faith and which is unmentioned in the New Testament.

Supposing that Rabbi J. had had some connection with this "third force," why was it not mentioned in the New Testament? Such skeptics as Voltaire and Frederick the Great noticed the striking similarity between the teaching of Rabbi J. and the doctrine of this sect. Was the secret sect an invention of Josephus?

Three

THE NARRATIVE OF FLAVIUS JOSEPHUS

Among the Jews," wrote Flavius Josephus in *The Jewish War*, "there are three schools of thought, whose adherents are called Pharisees, Sadducees, and Essenes respectively. The Essenes profess a severer discipline: they are Jews by birth and are peculiarly attached to each other.

"Of the two schools named first, the Pharisees are held to be the most authoritative exponents of the Law and count as the leading sect. They ascribe everything to Fate or to God: the decision whether or not to do right rests mainly with men, but in every action Fate takes some part. Every soul is incorruptible, but only the souls of good men pass into other bodies, the souls of bad men being subjected to eternal punishment. The Sadducees, the second order, deny Fate altogether and hold that God is incapable of either committing sin or seeing it; they say that men are free to choose between good and evil, and each individual must decide which he will follow. The permanence of the soul, punishments in Hades, and rewards they deny utterly."[1]

In other words, according to this description, too, the Rabbi's real opponents ought to have been the Sadducees, who rejected everything that we look on as Christian. But since Rabbi J. attacked mainly the Pharisees, we also ought to be able to discover differences

35

between the Pharisees and the Essenes—so long as we are sticking to the premise that the Rabbi may have had some connection with the Essenes. Josephus enumerates three such differences: the Essenes' strict ethics, their monastic life, and their doctrine of the immortality of the soul, which can be traced back to Gentile influences.

"It is indeed their unshakable conviction that bodies are corruptible and the material composing them impermanent, whereas souls remain immortal for ever. Coming forth from the most rarefied ether they are trapped in the prison-house of the body as if drawn down by one of nature's spells; but once freed from the bonds of the flesh, as if released after years of slavery, they rejoice and soar aloft. Teaching the same doctrines as the sons of Greece, they declare that for the good souls there waits a home beyond the ocean. . . . Bad souls they consign to a darksome, stormy abyss, full of punishments that know no end. . . .

"They tell these tales firstly because they believe souls to be immortal, and secondly in the hope of encouraging virtue and discouraging vice, since the good become better in their lifetime through the hope of a reward after death, and the propensies of the bad are restrained by the fear that, even if they are not caught in this life, after their dissolution they will undergo eternal punishment. This then is the religious teaching of the Essenes about the soul, providing an inescapable inducement to those who have once tasted their wisdom."

For nearly two thousand years these ideas of the Essenes and the Christian doctrine of the immortality of the soul have been connected with the concept, quite alien to the Old Testament, that life on earth is a trial and a journey on the way to eternal bliss. The Old Testament makes no mention of the immortality of the soul in this form nor of a domain of eternal bliss. What we normally call a later Hellenistic addition to Christianity emerges here as part of the ideology of a Jewish sect that existed before Rabbi J. was born. The concept that the body is only the prison of the soul, which is unknown in the Old Testament, also occurs among the Essenes according to Josephus.

Because of these beliefs the rules of the Essenes are against the physical and sensual side of life, and the things of this world: "They eschew pleasure-seeking as a vice and regard temperance and mastery of the passions as a virtue. Scorning wedlock . . . contemptuous of wealth, they are communists to perfection, and none of them will be found to be better off than the rest. . . . Showing indignation only when justified, they keep their tempers under control; they champion good faith and serve the cause of peace. Every word they speak is more binding than an oath; swearing they reject as something worse than perjury. . . . [a novice says that] he will ever love truth and seek to convict liars, will keep his hands from stealing, his soul innocent of unholy gain . . . they abstain from seventh-day work more rigidly than any other Jews . . . they do not venture to remove any utensil or to go and ease themselves.

"They are wonderfully devoted to the work of ancient writers, choosing mostly books that can help soul and body; from them in their anxiety to cure disease they learn all about medicinal roots and the properties of stones."

The German word *Heiland* (meaning savior but with connotations of healing) has a strange connection with the Essenes. The name Essenes or Essaeans is reminiscent of the Aramaic-Assyrian word *Assya*, which means doctor. A distinguishing mark of Rabbi J. was to heal and help the sick, and he ordered his disciples to continue this work.

According to Josephus, the community of the Essenes, which had about four thousand members[2] altogether, existed in two forms. The ascetic branch lived according to strict rules as a monastic community, whereas the other Essenes could live in towns and villages, and get married like ordinary citizens.

"They possess no one city but everywhere have large colonies. When adherents arrive from elsewhere, all local resources are put at their disposal as if they were their own, and men they have never seen before entertain them like old friends. And so when they travel they carry no baggage at all, but only weapons to keep off bandits."

Consequently the following instruction could easily come from the rules of the Essenes: "Take nothing for your journey, neither staves, nor scrip, neither bread, neither money. . . . And whatsoever house ye enter into, there abide, and thence depart. And whosoever will not receive you, when ye go out of that city, shake off the very dust from your feet for a testimony against them. And they departed, and went through the towns, preaching the gospel, and healing every where."[3]

Yet this quotation does not come from the Essenes: it is an order given to his disciples by Rabbi J. in the gospel according to St. Luke: to mention but one of many parallels.

The Essenes' monastic community was governed by special rules. As in Christian monastic orders there were various grades of membership corresponding to various degrees of enlightenment of the kind found in mystery religions. Everyone who entered the monastery gave his belongings to it: "Each man's possessions go into the pool and as with brothers their entire property belongs to them all. . . . Men to supervise the community's affairs are elected by show of hands, chosen for their tasks by universal suffrage."

It was probably much the same among Rabbi J.'s disciples, and we know the administrator of the communal purse. He was Judas, for "he . . . had the bag, and bare what was put therein."[4]

The Essenes' day was split up into specific periods for work, ritual ablutions, and meals, which were begun and ended by a special grace. "They show devotion to the Deity in a way all their own. Before the sun rises they do not utter a word on secular affairs, but offer to Him some traditional prayers as if beseeching him to appear. After this their supervisors send every man to the craft he understands best, and they work assiduously until an hour before noon, when they again meet in one place and donning linen loincloths wash all over with cold water. Thus purified they assemble in a building of their own which no one outside their community is allowed to enter: they go into the refectory as if it was a holy temple and sit down in silence. . . . The priest says grace before meat: to taste the food before this prayer is forbidden. After breakfast he offers a second prayer; for at beginning and end they give thanks to God as the Giver of Life. Then removing their garments as sacred they go back to their work till evening. Returning once more they take supper in the same way, seating their guests beside them if any have arrived. Neither shouting nor disorder ever desecrates the house: in conversation each gives way to his neighbor in turn. . . .

"Persons desirous of joining the sect are not immediately admitted. Excluded for a whole year, a man is required to observe the same rule of life as the members. . . . When in this period he has given proof of his temperance, he is associated more closely with the rule and permitted to share the purer waters of sanctification, though not yet admitted to the communal life. He has demonstrated his strength of purpose, but for two more years his character is tested, and if then he is seen to be worthy he is accepted into the society. But before touching the communal food he must swear terrible oaths . . . that he will ever hate the wicked and cooperate with the good . . . will never hide anything from members of the sect or reveal any of their secrets to others, even if brought by violence to the point of death. He further swears to impart their teaching to no man otherwise than as he himself received it . . . and to preserve the books of the sect and in the same way the names of the angels (messengers). Such are the oaths by which they make sure of their converts."

That is an abbreviated version of Flavius Josephus's story, and we wonder how he knew all this if the Essenes were really such a secret sect. A biographical note solves the puzzle. As a nineteen-year-old he actually belonged to the Essenes for three years, before he was arrested during a rebellion by the Romans, in whose service he then wrote *The Jewish War*.

Strictly speaking, Josephus did not betray anything that an outsider could not have found out. There is not a word about the books of the sect and its "angels" (the Greek word for messenger), not a word about where the Essenes' monastery was.

But what he does tell us contains many striking parallels with the New Testament—the sharing of possessions by the disciples and later by the early church in Jerusalem, and the pooling of property by the Essenes; the communal meals and the special kind of grace, the only sign by which the disciples recognized the resurrected Christ at Emmaus; the sect's ritual rules for purification and the baptism performed by John, which is simply called "purifying" in some passages in the Bible[5]; the rejection of swearing, "But let your communication be, Yea, yea; Nay, nay: for whatsoever is more than these cometh of evil"[6]; and lastly, *inter alia*, the ethic of loving one's neighbor, connected with the concept of a heavenly tribunal decreeing rewards and punishments for the immortal soul, an ethic which Philo of Alexandria describes even more clearly than Josephus: "The Essenes have been brought together by their zeal for rectitude and the passionateness of their love of humanity."[7]

So it is not surprising that down the centuries there have always been theologians who believed that Rabbi J. was an Essene. As early as 1792 the theologian Karl Friedrich Bahrdt[8] wrote in his *Letters to Truth-seeking Readers* that J. was connected with the Essenes through Nicodemus (in the third chapter of St. John) and Joseph of Arimathea. Bahrdt also noticed that J. used "two kinds of discourse" so as not to transgress the role of secrecy.

The Age of Enlightenment used the Essenes to explain some of the miracles. Certain scholars asserted that the crucifixion and resurrection were only a theatrical production staged by the Essenes and consequently that the white-clad youth who announced the resurrection to the women in the empty tomb was simply one of the Essenes, who, as is well known, wore white clothes. A hundred years ago the white robe of the Essenes inspired another theologian to explain that Rabbi J. was the son of an Essene youth to whom Mary had given herelf in an ecstasy, because she had taken him for an angel in his white raiment.[9] The child had then been handed over to the order, which was quite usual according to Josephus's account.

August Friedrich Gförer, born zu Calw, student at the Tübingen Foundation and curate of Stuttgart, wrote in 1831: "The Christian church emerged from the Essene community, whose ideas it developed, and its organization would be inexplicable without the Essenes' rules."[10]

Theology and the church did not take up these ideas

of liberal theologians because they saw in them an attempt to undermine the uniqueness of J.'s life and teaching. No one was prepared to admit more than a vague resemblance between the accounts of Josephus, Philo, and the New Testament, and with some reason. For the Essenes are not mentioned once in the New Testament, not a single text of the Essenes had been handed down, and no one knew where the Essenes' monastery might have been located, if indeed it had ever existed.

Pliny is the only person to make a brief reference to it: "The Essenes have withdrawn a considerable distance from the west shore of the Dead Sea to be sheltered from its deleterious effects—a solitary community living without women that has renounced every contact with Venus and money, and whose only companions are the palm trees. . . . At their feet once lay the town of Engeddi. . . . On the other side lies Massada, a fortress on a rock, not far from the Dead Sea."[11]

No Essene monastery has ever been found there, and we may well doubt whether Pliny's geography was very strong, for Massada does not lie on the other side, but on the same shore as Ein Gedi, as Engeddi is written today. And there are palm trees by the Dead Sea not only at Ein Gedi, but also some twenty miles farther north at Ain Feshka, not far from the mouth of the Jordan near Jericho, where in the midst of a lifeless stony desert right on the Dead Sea frogs still sit croaking in the channels of a clear freshwater spring.

So if Pliny's poetic observation that palm trees were their only companions is right, the only possible sites for a settlement on the west shore of the Dead Sea are those two places where a spring emerges from the fissured rock, twelve hundred feet below sea level.

But there was no one like Schliemann, who took Homer literally and discovered Troy, to take Pliny's details seriously and search for and find the Essenes' monastery. For nineteen hundred years Josephus, Philo, and Pliny were suspected of being Oriental storytellers, until the secret books of the Essenes—the famous Dead Sea Scrolls—were discovered by chance in the Qumran caves not far from Ain Feshka.

Four

THE PROOF THAT
CAME LATER

T was not the actual discovery of the Dead Sea scrolls that formed one of the most exciting chapters in modern archeology, but the attempts of scholars to acquire the irreplaceable documents from the Arab desert nomads and their intermediaries by haggling, bribery, and trickery—often risking their lives in the process—to prevent their destruction by the hazards of war, ignorance, or disappointed money lust.

It all began when fifteen-year-old Mohammed ad Dhib, of the Taamirah tribe,[1] bored while keeping his sheep, threw some stones into one of the narrow caves that abound on the steep slopes around the Dead Sea. According to other reports he was looking for a lost sheep when he found the cave. Be that as it may, Mohammed heard a clinking noise instead of stone striking stone, and he rushed away in panic-stricken fear of evil spirits.

The next morning he had calmed down and decided to go with a friend to collect the gold treasure hoard that he suspected was there. They were bitterly disappointed when all they found were a few earthenware vessels and some old leather scrolls. They took one of them back to camp and unrolled it until it reached from one side of the tent to the other, as they later recounted in amazement. It was one of the scrolls that later cost a quarter of a million dollars to buy and which is now on display in the Shrine of the Book in Jerusalem.

The Bedouins did not know what to make of them, and one day took a couple of scrolls to Bethlehem to Chalil Iskandar Shahin, a Syrian Christian, who ran a grocery-cum-cobbler's shop, and was known as Kando. Kando was not interested, but as the old material might come in handy for mending shoes, he kept the leather scrolls. (The very thought that the oldest extant manuscript of the Bible might have been used piecemeal for soling shoes is still enough to make any scholar's heart stop beating.)

Later, when Kando examined the scrolls more closely, he got the impression that they might be more than the usual fake antiquities and took one to the Syrian Monastery of St. Mark in the Old City of Jerusalem. Perhaps the Metropolitan would be interested in old documents. But the Metropolitan did not appreciate the value of the scrolls, either, and began to offer fragments to various institutions for examination, after he had taken a supply of scrolls from Kando on commission for a few shillings.

So far the story of the discovery can still be reconstructed fairly reliably. But the confusion of war before the founding of the state of Israel in 1948, the compulsion to keep absolute secrecy about the finds, which automatically belonged to the state by law as archeological material and could not be traded in, and the partition of the country into an Arab and a Jewish sector, explain why no two stories coincide.

Basically two stories of the same discovery can be

distinguished.[2] One of them tells how the Hebrew University in the Israeli sector of Jerusalem came upon the scrolls, and the other how in the Arab sector of the city the American Oriental Institute and the Dominican Archeological-Theological Institute on the one hand and the Jordanian Government Archeological Office in Amman on the other tried more or less legally to do business with the suspicious Bedouins.

In both versions Kando of Bethlehem and the Syrian Metropolitan of St. Mark's Monastery in Jerusalem are the shadowy key figures. They possessed seven scrolls, whose value they did not even suspect, and offered them to one prospective purchaser after another, each of whom thought that he was the first person to hear about the finds.

Thus the Israeli archeologist Dr. Sukenik of the Hebrew University tells us that on November 23, 1947, an unknown Armenian showed him a fragment of a scroll for the first time. It was an extraordinary situation. Dr. Sukenik stood on one side of the barbed-wire fence the British Military Government had erected around the Hebrew University as a protection against the Arabs, the Armenian on the other. Across the barbed wire Sukenik heard about the finds by the Dead Sea. He checked the piece of leather and the characters. They really were of great antiquity.

A few days later, on the twenty-eighth, the United Nations in New York was to decide on Palestine's future. It was a foregone conclusion that there would be a war between Arabs and Jews if the UN decided on the foundation of the state of Israel. When Dr. Sukenik

47

heard over the radio that the UN had postponed its decision for a day, he seized the last opportunity to travel to nearby Bethlehem with the Armenian a few hours before the outbreak of war.

While hour after hour went by, Dr. Sukenik sat with the Armenian and some Arab merchants in a tumbledown building in Bethlehem and haggled at Oriental length. Gradually the Arabs became less suspicious and let Sukenik see at least two scrolls and a clay vessel. Once again precious minutes passed. At last he had progressed so far that he was allowed to take the scrolls to Jerusalem for examination. While he breathlessly compared the new scrolls with others to determine their age and contents, he heard the news of the partitioning of Palestine over the radio. The state of Israel was founded, war began, the other scrolls were lost to him, and Bethlehem became a part of Jordan.

Meanwhile the Syrian Metropolitan offered his scrolls to the American Oriental Institute in the Jordanian sector of Jerusalem. In February 1948 he told the institute over the telephone that he had found some old scrolls in the library of his monastery. Dr. Trever, who was acting as director of the institute at the time, showed interest, and the scrolls were brought to him next day in an old chest. The first rapid comparison with other old Hebrew manuscripts electrified Trever, for the writing on the leather scrolls was even older. There before him was the oldest copy of the Book of Isaiah, centuries older than the hitherto known texts. Trever was given permission to take photocopies of the scrolls—and only then did the Metropolitan admit that the scrolls were not from his monastery, but had been found somewhere in a cave about a year before. The location of the cave was still the secret of the Bedouins.

The Metropolitan took the scrolls away with him and smuggled them into America, ostensibly to save them from the hazards of war, but probably to sell them there for a high price. When Sukenik heard about it, he wrote in his diary: "The Jewish people have lost a precious heritage."

But it was not lost. The Metropolitan could not find a buyer. The photocopies taken by Trever had been published, so that acquisition of the originals was not absolutely imperative. Seven years later, in 1954, Sukenik's son, Yigael Yadin, who became famous for his excavation of the mountain fortress of Massada, was on a lecture tour of the United States. One day he received a telephone call from a journalist, who told him to read next day's *Wall Street Journal*. In it he found a small unobtrusive advertisement saying that four Dead Sea scrolls were for sale. Yadin at once made contact with the Metropolitan's agent through intermediaries. Neither knew who the other was. They agreed on a price of a quarter of a million dollars, which Yigael Yadin soon raised through friends and a guarantee from the Israeli government.

On July 1, 1954, the four scrolls were taken from the Waldorf-Astoria Hotel in New York to the Israeli Embassy in a large black chest. Seven years after their discovery, the scrolls were back in Israel. Professor Sukenik never knew about it—he had died the year before —and the Metropolitan did not find out to whom he had sold the scrolls until a year later.

Let us go back to 1948. Neither Professor Sukenik nor the American Oriental Institute had admitted knowing anything about the scrolls or that they were desperately looking for the caves in order to prove the authenticity of the documents. But the American Institute had photocopies of some of the scrolls and decided to publish them. On April 11, 1948, a whole year after their discovery, Millar Burrows, the director of the institute, told the world at large of the discovery of a manuscript of the Bible that was a thousand years older than any previously known copy.

But owing to an editorial lapse, the report said that the scrolls had been found in the Monastery of St. Mark in Jerusalem. Sukenik knew better and so he wrote a letter to the editor of the newspaper saying that the scrolls had been found near the Dead Sea. Burrows read this correction by chance in the *Rome Daily American* of April 28 on his way back to the United States, when his ship docked in Genoa, and he also learned for the first time that not only his institute, but also the Hebrew University, barely two miles away, possessed parts of the scrolls. But he was still better off than Lancaster Harding, the director of the Jordanian Government Archeological Office in Amman. Not until November 1948, when he read about it in a scholarly journal, did he learn that one of the most astonishing discoveries ever had been made in his country eighteen months before.

There was no question of keeping things secret now; the Dead Sea scrolls had hit the headlines, although no one knew where the cave was.

Lancaster Harding visited the Monastery of St. Mark, hoping to find out the location of the cave. Risking death from the fire of Israeli snipers, he reached the monastery in the narrow lanes of the old part of Jerusalem. In the meantime the Metropolitan had been told the exact location by Kando and had secretly organized an illegal search of the cave. By chance Harding met an old monk in the monastery whom he questioned about the matter and who, before anyone could stop him, described the approximate site of the discovery. The cave ought to be somewhere south of the spot where the road from Jerusalem forks to Jericho and the Dead Sea in the Jordanian depression.

There were hundreds of caves in the porous stone of this region and it seemed unlikely that anyone would rediscover a specific cave that Mohammed had only stumbled on by chance after two thousand years. Lancaster Harding tried to recruit Bedouins for the search, but they refused for fear they might become involved with the police.

And so it was that a Belgian observer for the United Nations set out on a seemingly hopeless search for the cave in January 1949, in the company of two soldiers of the Arab Legion and a Jordanian captain. After three days the cave was rediscovered for the second time in two years.

It lay between the mouth of the Jordan and the spring of Ain Feshka, not far from the ruins of Qumran, a settlement on the shores of the Dead Sea that has been abandoned for centuries. They found remains and fragments of the scrolls and were able to determine from other finds that the scrolls and earthenware vessels dated to a period close to the birth of Christ and were not, as many people suspected, from a medieval hiding place.

But who had hidden the scrolls? Only two scrolls reproduced an Old Testament text. They were two different, well-preserved copies of the Book of Isaiah, one published by Sukenik, the other by Burrows. As both scrolls tally with the text of Isaiah that we know, even down to a few unimportant variations, the theologians happily accepted them as a confirmation of the Christian tradition and saw no need for any revision of Christian dogma or principles.

The other scrolls did not concern the theologians. They were not biblical texts, but scriptures hitherto unknown from any other translation or manuscript. There were commentaries on the prophets Habakkuk, Micah, and Zephaniah, and a scroll of hymns or psalms of thanksgiving in which familiar quotations about awaiting the end of the world were commented on. There was mention of a Teacher of Righteousness and of the Sons of Light, who had withdrawn into the desert, and of the sons of the Sons of Darkness, who had been led astray by froward priests. They were mainly apocalyptic scriptures, whose authors could not be determined with certainty. Nevertheless, it was remarkable that many words and ideas from these unknown scrolls reappeared almost word for word in the New Testament.

The decisive document that made identification possible was the so-called Manual of Discipline. Everything that had previously only been known from the descriptions of Josephus reappeared here, although not word for word and with some variation of detail. The Essenes' library had been found, but there was no trace of an Essene monastery.

After the rediscovery of the cave, there was calm again by the Dead Sea. The only visitors were the Taamirah Bedouins, who, accompanied by their flocks, made their way through the region in spring when the mountain wilderness showed a trace of greenery. And once again it was these Bedouins who discovered the second cave in 1952. The haggling over every square inch of the scrolls began again, and adventure stories could be written about it. Then archeologists found a third cave.

Next, two hundred caves were systematically examined, often at the risk of the searchers' lives. Within a radius of a few miles round Qumran they found a dozen more hiding places with scrolls, household utensils, and coins. Some of the texts were written in secret script; others were compilations of references to the Messiah. The "New Covenant," which Luther translated as "New Testament," was also mentioned, and there was constant reference to the Teacher of Righteousness. (As many scrolls are hard to open, some of the texts have not yet been deciphered.) Incidentally, Qumran is a place that had already attracted the attention of archeologists in the last century. As the word Qumran is pronounced by the Arabs like Gomorrah, and both words have gmr (or qu-m-r-n) as their consonantal stem, which is the only one that matters in Semitic languages, scholars had the idea of looking for the biblical Gomorrah there. (The modern view is that the Gomorrah that perished by fire lies at the other end of the Dead Sea near Sodom.)

Archeologists were stimulated to make these early excavations by a ruined area—the name Kirbeth Qumran means simply the ruins of Qumran — in which scholars soon recognized the foundations of the walls of a Roman castle that controlled the beginning of the road to the western shore of the Dead Sea in a strategically favorable spot. In other words, it was a stronghold similar to the fortress of Machaerus, on the opposite shore, in which John the Baptist was held prisoner by Herod.

When the first cave was rediscovered in 1949, superficial digs were made in various parts of the ruined area, but nothing special was found. Not until two years later, at the end of 1951, did Lancaster Harding of the Jordanian Government Archeological Office and Pater de Vaux, director of the Dominican Archeological-Theological Institute in Jerusalem, decide to excavate at Qumran yet once more.

For five years, during the comparatively cool winter months, they excavated at Kirbeth Qumran in a landscape of terrible solitude. They found a cemetery with more than a thousand graves, in which only men were buried. They found a room with more than a thousand beakers, bowls, plates, and dishes, and next to it a large refectory, in which the president's seat was marked by tiles; they found workshops for artisans, cisterns, and baths for ritual purification. They found a writing room with a huge wooden table and two inkwells—the scriptorium in which the majority of the texts found in the nearby caves were probably written. Coins and potsherds found in the caves and at Qumran proved the connection. The Essenes' monastery had been found.

Not far from the spot where John the Baptist, the voice crying in the wilderness, preached repentance to mankind and where Rabbi J. himself was baptized, not far from the place where tradition has it that he withdrew into the wilderness for forty days and forty nights and was tempted, not far from Jericho, the oldest city in the world and the first city that the children of Israel conquered in the promised land after forty years of wandering in the wilderness, not far from the place where the patriarch Moses is buried, in the middle of a landscape of terrible beauty, lies Qumran, the monastery of the Essene monks. In this monastery, long before Rabbi J.'s birth, ideas were written down that occurred later in his teaching and revolutionized the world. Is Qumran the "cradle of Christianity"?

THE SONS OF LIGHT

Concepts and ideas have their history, too. When John the Baptist preached repentance in the wilderness because the kingdom of God was at hand, it was not his own doctrine. As much as two hundred years before him, especially devout Jews (the Hebrew word for them is Chasidim, accent on the last syllable) had believed that the end of the world and the kingdom of God were near, for "there were evil people in Israel at this time," it says in the First Book of Maccabees, "who persuaded the people, saying, Let us make a covenant with the heathen around us and accept their religion; for we have had to suffer much since the day when we separated from the heathen."[1]

The children of Israel had always suffered at the hands of the heathens, i.e., those who were not Jews. They got to know them as occupying powers. After the captivity in Babylon came the Persian empire; after the Persians, whom Alexander the Great defeated in 333 B.C., came the Greeks. When Alexander died, his empire was divided up among the Diadochi after lengthy struggles. At first it was the Ptolemies in Egypt who drew the Jewish territory into their sphere of dominion. In 200 B.C., the Syrian branch of the Diadochi, the Seleucids, succeeded in taking over the power in Judaea. When the Seleucid ruler Antiochus IV ascended the throne in 175 B.C. and installed a Greek cult in the Temple at Jerusalem, the Jews rebelled. Under Judas Maccabeus they fought against the heathens and their Greek-influenced religions, whereas others, resigned after centuries of foreign dominion, voted for acceptance of the foreign religions out of political opportunism.

The Chasidim protested against the sinfulness of their day, and because they were persecuted they left the villages and towns and retreated to the desert of Judaea between Jerusalem and the Dead Sea, where they hid in caves.[2] They were the forerunners of the Essenes. There they awaited the coming of the kingdom of God, while leading lives of the strictest orthodoxy.

But while one group of Chasidim clung to their expectation of the end in spite of all their disappointments, others became skeptical and separated from the original movement. That gave them their name, for the word *pharisee* means simply "separated one." Already in the New Testament we can sense the skepticism of the Pharisees when the coming of the kingdom is mentioned—and that is the reason why John the Baptist attacked them so vehemently as a generation of vipers. Kurt Schubert writes as follows: "The most important element in the controversy between the newly arisen Phariseeism and the priestly radicals of Qumran was the preaching of the end of the world. The Pharisees refused to recognize the various apocalyptic pronouncements as inspired."[3]

That is why there are books in the Old Testament "that are not considered equal to the Holy Scriptures and are yet useful and good to read," as Luther defined the Apocrypha, the Old Testament books which were not accepted in the canon, the recognized list of genuine books. They consist mainly of those books and prophets who foretold the end of the world—the very books and prophets that are constantly quoted in the Essenes' scrolls.

So the Essenes had their own tradition in addition to the canonical scriptures. Their canon was larger than that of the Pharisees, enriched by those prophets of the hope which the others had resigned themselves to rejecting.

On the one hand the Chasidic Essenes were strictly orthodox and so more Jewish than other Jews. They, too, like the Sadducees, traced themselves back to Zadok, the high priest, and their monastic life had a markedly priestly orientation. On the other hand these chosen among the chosen people had become cut off from the tradition and development of Judaism down the centuries owing to their fixation on a past historical situation—the profanation of the temple in the time of Antiochus. They were conservatives, rooted in their own historical past, not that of the Jewish people.

To the Essenes the temple at Jerusalem was still corrupted by sacrilege. They did not even turn toward the temple to pray; in the temple the Sons of Darkness reigned, but they, the Sons of Light, prayed in the opposite direction, toward the east, where the sun rose.

And so the Essenes gave themselves a name which was based on a concept unknown to the rest of Judaism. They called themselves the Sons of Light, who fought against the froward priests and the Sons of Darkness.

The so-called War Scroll that was found in the first cave describes in detail the struggle of the Sons of Light at the end of time: "To the understanding: the order of the war. The first engagement of the Sons of Light against the Sons of Darkness . . . when the Sons of Light who are now in exile return from the 'desert of the nations' to pitch camp in the desert of Judah."[4] The Manual of Discipline, the rules of the Essene monks, also says that it is a duty: "to love all the Sons of Light each according to his stake in the formal community of God; and to hate all the Sons of Darkness, each one according to the measure of his guilt, which God will ultimately requite."[5]

Light and darkness are continually occurring as antithetical synonyms for truth and godlessness: "The origin of truth lies in the Fountain of Light and that of perversity in the Wellspring of Darkness."[6]

And even people who only remember the Bible vaguely think that they are rereading it when it says in the Manual of Discipline: "All that is and ever was comes from a God of knowledge. Before things came into existence, he determined the plan of them."[7] This verse in the Manual of Discipline comes immediately before the passage in which the light is called the truth. The celebrated mystical and mysterious prologue at the beginning of the gospel according to St. John uses very similar language to express identical ideas: "In the beginning was the Word, and the Word was with God, and the Word was God. The same was in the beginning with God. All things were made by him; and without him was not any thing that was made. In him was life; and the life was the light of men. And the light shineth in the darkness; and the darkness comprehended it not."[8]

Here the New Testament and the Essenes' secret doctrine meet, here the faith of an orthodox Jewish sect encounters the Jew who called his disciples children of light and himself the light of the world.

Is Qumran the "cradle of Christianity" and is Christianity nothing but the historical development of the teaching of Chasidic hermits, who, angered by a Seleucid king, vainly awaited the end of the world and the coming of the Messiah in the desert? To put it theologically, did Rabbi J. have a personal revelation, or was he merely the skillful propagandist of a long-established sect and its doctrine?

Until the Dead Sea scrolls were published in 1948 we could only speculate about this possibility. The writings of the New Testament and the accounts of Josephus and Philo were known. They suggested a connection, but they did not prove anything.

That has changed since we have known the texts of the Essene community by the Dead Sea. Now we can compare individual sentences from different documents; we can put the New Testament alongside the Essenes' texts and examine them.

Moreover, we know that the Essene texts are older than the New Testament scriptures. That is proved by comparing the characters, by the scientifically demonstrable age of the scrolls, and especially by the fact that Qumran was destroyed in the year 70, at the same time as the temple in Jerusalem—the coins confirm this —and that the accounts of the New Testament were not finished until after the year 70.

Now if a comparison of New Testament and Qumran manuscripts shows that not only a similarity but also a direct dependence in individual words, ideas, and doctrine exists—then no amount of pious faith and counterargument is of any use. It is an undeniable fact that Rabbi J. took over the Qumran doctrine, possibly altering and concentrating it, but that he is not the creator of the doctrine we ascribe to him.

The conceivable alternative explanation that it was the evangelists and St. Paul who subsequently used Qumran ideas and put them into Rabbi J.'s mouth, does not improve matters. If we can still prove that Christianity and its doctrine as expressed in the Bible are Essene-inspired, it means merely that Christianity does not stem from Rabbi J. but from later interpreters, and so the dependence of the Christian faith on the monks of Qumran must be equally admitted, unless we decide to reject wholesale the finds of otherwise valid scholarship.

So far I have mentioned only one—perhaps chance —example of striking similarity, and I realize that the reader will expect a number of other examples before he can form an opinion. But I should say that it is only the first of many which I shall quote later.

First we must ask ourselves whether the evangelists —whatever their reasons may have been—say anything to show that it was physically and geographically possible for Rabbi J. to have met the people from Qumran.

We can read in Matthew and Mark that John the Baptist appeared in the Judaean desert and baptized in the Jordan and "there went out unto him all the land of Judaea, and they of Jerusalem, and were all baptized of him. . . .'"[9] St. John describes the place more specifically as east of the Jordan near Bethabara (Bethany).[10]

Today a memorial church stands on this very spot in the no-man's-land between Jordan and Israel, some five miles east of Jericho and also some five miles from the place where the Jordan flows into the Dead Sea. It is the next place from which one can reach the Jordan from Jerusalem. From Jerusalem one can see the Dead Sea lying far below. If you stand on the hill beneath which Jericho, the oldest city in the world with its legendary walls, lies buried—and at one point you can look back into the Stone Age down a shaft beside the walls—then you look across the date palms of the oasis of Jericho to the Jordan and the place where John baptized people. Less than two hours on foot across dull lifeless scree and you reach the place where the voice crying in the wilderness preached, where today the Jerusalem road leads through a ford to Bethany.

If you look out from Jericho to the opposite side, your guidebook explains that there high up on the mountainside is, according to tradition, the place where Rabbi J. was tempted by the devil in solitude after his baptism. That would mean that after his baptism he must have hurried to Jericho and gone into the mountainous wilderness on the far side of the town.

But if you stand on the site of Jericho and look neither left at the Jordan nor right at the Mountain of the Temptation, but straight ahead, you have the dull glitter of the Dead Sea ahead of you, framed by the grayish-brown mountains of the Judaean desert. And it is just there, behind the first mountain spurs on the Dead Sea, remote from the world in a lifeless desert and yet only ten miles away, that the Essene monastery of Qumran stands. From Qumran you can see the site where John baptized, and Machaerus, the fortress in which he was beheaded. Now as in the past there is nothing but desert in between, because there are no springs. For centuries Bethany, Jericho, and Qumran have been the only oases far and wide, and at the point of intersection of the three towns lies the baptismal site, close to the lowest point on the surface of the earth.

Why should not the place to which he withdrew for forty days and forty nights have been near Qumran, seeing that the hermit John would scarcely have lived in a town like Jericho or Bethany, but might easily have inhabited one of the caves around Qumran, for even a hermit needs water occasionally?

I find it very odd that Rabbi J. came to the Jordan simply to be baptized, summoned by John the Baptist's call to repentance, and then went straight back to Galilee, as suggested by the erroneous translation of the "third day," on which he is supposed to have been in Cana for the marriage.

There is yet another passage which generally passes unnoticed because it seems to be only a minor detail in a more important story. Unlike the other evangelists, St. John tells us that Rabbi J. appointed his first disciples the day after his baptism in Judaea. In this story there is a passage which could just as well have been omitted, if we assume that it was only a matter of the enrollment of the first disciples. It reads as follows: "Again the day after, John stood and two of his disciples. And looking upon J. as he walked, he saith, Behold the Lamb of God! And the two disciples heard him speak, and they followed J. . . . Then J. turned, and saw them following, and saith unto them, What seek ye? They said unto him, Rabbi [which is to say, being interpreted, Master], where dwellest thou? He saith unto them, Come and see. They came and saw where he dwelt, and abode with him that day: for it was about the tenth hour."[11]

In retrospect we may take it for a pleasant adornment—but the question is why on earth the first thing that the two disciples asked, when they heard that the Lamb of God was passing by, was where he lived. Or, if we work from the theory that the evangelists subsequently invented material that had no foundation in fact, what made John mention (but not explain) an unnecessary detail of that kind, if it did not have a special meaning? Might we not have expected a sentence such as "And the three of them walked together to Jericho"? And the question is not answered; if anything it is further obscured by the time mentioned, "the tenth hour" (4 P.M.). This time reference may have had a meaning for initiates. For example, the fact that strangers to Qumran were admitted to the evening meal, but not to the midday meal, as Josephus says. This time would have little meaning if it referred to a visit to Rabbi J. in a secular district such as Jericho.

Apart from tradition, what is there to say that Rabbi J. did not live in one of the caves in or around Qumran?

There is another point. When the Rabbi was in the wilderness, "[he] was with wild beasts; and the angels ministered unto him."[12] In various languages, Greek for example, messenger and angel are the same word, and the Essenes had a characteristic "angelic doctrine" that had to be kept secret. What is there against Rabbi J. having spent his "novitiate" in a cave outside Qumran, as Josephus described postulants doing? Then the "angels" would have been messengers from Qumran. Since the Essenes are not mentioned in the New Testament for a definite reason, this brief reference to unspecified "angels" could be left in, in spite of all the other "editing": "He who hath ears to hear, let him hear."

I admit that one has to have seen with one's own eyes how close together the baptismal site and Qumran are in the terrifying expanse of barren mountains to be able to connect them with an inner logic that goes beyond the purely geographic evidence. Nevertheless, why precisely Qumran and not Jericho, Bethany, or a place on the banks of the Jordan?

The answer is again geographical, but this time with a "theological" justification as well. It depends on how we accentuate one particular sentence in the Bible so as to extract a quite different meaning from it.

T HE account of John the Baptist and the Rabbi's baptism is one of the few passages in the New Testament where the four evangelists tell the same story, although with considerable variation. (The only material common to all four gospels consists of J.'s baptism, the number of disciples, the story of the passion, but not the Last Supper, one "miracle"—the feeding of the four or five thousand—and the psychologically interesting information that the Rabbi *could not* perform miracles in his home town.)

John the Baptist plays a leading part in the Rabbi's biography. J. receives his ministry at the time of his baptism by John. It is the Baptist who, according to one account, calls him Messiah, and according to another suspects him to be the Messiah and lets him be questioned by his disciples. Rabbi J. does not begin his mission until after the Baptist's arrest.

The Baptist was looked on by his contemporaries as the reincarnation of Elijah, for in the Book of Malachi we find the sentence: "Behold, I will send you Elijah the prophet before the coming of the great and dreadful day of the Lord."[1] John the Baptist, whom we also know as "the voice of one crying in the wilderness," preached this day of the Lord, as Matthew, for example, describes him:

"In these days came John the Baptist, preaching in the wilderness of Judaea, And saying, Repent ye: for the kingdom of heaven is at hand. For this is he that was spoken of by the prophet Esaias, saying, The voice of one crying in the wilderness, Prepare ye the way of the Lord, make his paths straight."[2]

The connection is illuminating. The man who summons men to repentance in the wilderness is the voice of one crying in the wilderness. And as the Baptist was considered to be the Rabbi's forerunner, it is perfectly logical for him to summon everyone to prepare for the coming of God's kingdom. Normally we link this preparation with baptism; it is the way of preparation. But it is possible to interpret the biblical passage about the preacher in the wilderness differently, as Shalom Ben Chorin writes:

"Although he is admittedly described as the voice of one crying in the wilderness (Matthew 3:2; Luke 3:4), there is an error in translation here that goes back to the Septuagint [the Greek translation of the Bible]. John is supposed to appear here as the fulfilment of Isaiah 40:3, the first chapter of the scripture of consolation coming from the Babylonian captivity. But following the punctuation of the cantilenas of the Masoretic text,[3] we really ought to read this passage as follows:

Voice of one crying:
In the wilderness
Make a way for the Lord.
Make straight in the desert
A highway for our God!"[4]

Thus the same words suddenly yield a completely new meaning. The general summons to prepare the way of the Lord is made specific. The way is not to be made just anywhere, but in the wilderness.

If we look up Isaiah in the Old Testament, now that our curiosity has been aroused, we find that all the old editions, beginning with Luther, read "the voice of one crying in the wilderness." The newly revised Lutheran Bible of 1964 is the first to render the passage in Isaiah 40:3, correctly:

"A voice cries: Prepare the way of the Lord in the wilderness. . . ."

Although the corresponding passage in the New Testament is a literal quotation from Isaiah, the revised Lutheran Bible still retains the same mistranslation in its version of the gospels:

"The voice of one crying in the wilderness, Prepare ye the way of the Lord. . . ."[5]

According to the now correct translation of the Old Testament, the way of the Lord is defined (it is to be built in the wilderness). According to the inaccurate New Testament translation, the Baptist is described (the voice of one crying in the wilderness). This is not the result of chance or accident.

When the Old Testament was translated into Greek by seventy translators—the Latin word for seventy, *septuaginta*, gave this edition its name—250 years before these events on the orders of an Egyptian king, the second filter began to function and inevitably altered and often distorted the original ideas, for every translation implies a transference into a new world of ideas and experience.

And the writers of the gospels, which were finished more than a generation after the death of Rabbi J., no longer lived in immediate expectation of the Messiah. For them the Messiah had already come; he had entered Jerusalem humbly on an ass. The idea that the way of the Lord had to be prepared in the wilderness and nowhere else no longer had any meaning for them. Nor had he come to them in the wilderness. The desert religion of Moses had emigrated from Palestine in the form of Christianity to countries where deserts were not a characteristic feature. Moses may have found the God of the old covenant in the wilderness, but the new covenant was sealed in Jerusalem.

So the message of John the Baptist with its specific reference to time and place became the timelessly true message of the coming of the Lord. The process of idealizing the message and the symbolization of mis-understood references began because historical reality had been forgotten.

In retrospect everything was referred to Christ, because other references did not seem to make sense. So, as the Hebrew text has no punctuation marks, the translators transferred the emphasis from the coming of the Lord in the wilderness to the preacher who lived in the wilderness. From being a Jewish sect in Palestine, Christianity began to become a world religion. The kingdom of God could begin anywhere, not only in the desert of the detested murderers of God. The translators mistranslated because they were thinking in terms of their time and their world, and not in those of the time and world of Rabbi J.

In Rabbi J.'s world there was nothing new or special about political malcontents and religious ascetics—their motives were often indistinguishable—withdrawing into the desert.

The chosen people's tradition of staying in the wilderness went much further back than the Chasidim. After the exodus from Egypt, the people of Israel had become God's people in the wilderness. And the man who has never been in the rocky Judaean desert or the Negev will find it hard to understand the irrational forces that the disturbing solitude and stillness of such a landscape can arouse. Not without reason did the first Christian monks seek God in the solitude of the desert.

Moreover, the situation of Qumran and the baptismal site in the Judaean desert is not fortuitous. From Qumran you can see Mount Nebo, the mountain from which, according to the Bible, Moses saw the promised land he himself was never to set foot in. Close to Qumran on the road to Jericho, legend locates the tomb of Moses, with whom God had spoken and made a covenant, the God from whom the people of Israel constantly backslid, beginning with the golden calf and continuing down to the time of the Maccabees, when foreign influences and foreign religions came into the country again under the Diadochi, who ruled after King Alexander of Macedon.

When the orthodox Chasidim went out into the Judaean desert to follow the law of Moses to the letter, they sought out the very place in the vast desert region between Beersheba and Jericho which was traditionally doubly connected with Moses, the founder of their faith. On the borders of the promised land that Moses saw, and near Jericho, the first town that the children of Israel conquered, they founded the monastery of Qumran in order to await the new covenant with God the Father there, as it says in the Essene Manual of Discipline. It was the same new covenant which Rabbi J. announced at the Last Supper and Luther translated as "New Testament."

We who were born later and are members of an alien culture forget all too easily, aided and abetted by theologians and priests, that the new covenant did not mean a new religion. The first Christians continued to pray in the temple at Jerusalem and required Rabbi J.'s followers to be circumcised and to follow the Mosaic law.

By the new covenant the Jews understood that God would embrace his chosen people again and would lead them to independence from their subjection to the occupying power, for the chosen people saw themselves not only as a religious but also as a political and national community. Whenever things went badly for the Jewish people, as in the Babylonian captivity, prophets such as Isaiah preached the savior from slavery, the Messiah, the one promised by God who was to be the "King of the Jews" and "Prince of Peace." As far as the Jewish people were concerned, the savior did not come to free them from sin, but to liberate them from foreign domination. When the God of

Abraham, Isaac, and Jacob helped his people, it meant that he had already forgiven the sin of apostasy.

The people from Qumran also believed in the Messiah, the savior from subjection to Rome, and many scholars think that the "Teacher of Righteousness" mentioned so often in the Dead Sea scrolls was one of the sect's first failed Messiahs.

In the Essenes' view, the temple religion was corrupt. They did not expect the Messiah and the new covenant with Yahweh to come from Jerusalem, but from among themselves, the Sons of Light, who had been preparing themselves for the coming of the Lord since the days of the Maccabees by leading a monastic life. Here, on the spot where Moses had seen the Promised Land, he would appear and conclude a new covenant.

And that is literally what we find in the Essenes' Manual of Discipline. To bring about the coming of God's kingdom, "they are to be kept apart from any consort with froward men, that they may indeed go into the wilderness to prepare the way, i.e., do what Scripture enjoins when it says: 'Prepare in the wilderness the way . . . make straight in the desert a highway for our God.' "[6]

And that is exactly what John the Baptist did and preached. The only thing is that now we understand what he meant. The Messiah was not to be expected from among the sacrilegious priests of corruption and the Children of Darkness, but from those who served the Lord in the wilderness, the Children of Light. That is the Baptist's real message. If Yahweh was to help his people, it was only because men like the Essenes, living apart from the froward men, followed the true Mosaic law. The renewed covenant and with it the savior and promised redeemer could only come from those who kept the old covenant. God was not preparing his kingdom in Jerusalem, but in the wilderness.

So was John the Baptist an Essene?

Millar Burrows, who played a decisive part in the publication of the scrolls but finds it quite painful to have to acknowledge similarities between the people of Qumran and Christianity, has to admit that there are certainly "many points in which John's ideas resemble those to be found in the Dead Sea scrolls. Like the Essenes he devoted himself to the task of preparing the way of the Lord in the wilderness. His baptism of repentance may have had a connection with the ritual baths of the Qumran sect; he emphasized as does the Manual of Discipline that without previous spiritual purification a bath in water cannot redeem a sin.

"Parallels have also been found between the Messianic expectations of John and those in the Dead Sea scrolls. His prophecy that the man who came after him would execute judgment by fire is undoubtedly related in some way with Zarathustra's idea of a world conflagration, which would finally melt the mountains and pour forth over the earth like a river, and this concept is vividly depicted in one of the Psalms of Thanksgiving—a Qumran scroll—in the images of the floods of Belial which will destroy even the foundations of the mountains in their flames. The concept of a Messianic baptism by the Holy Ghost also occurs in

74

the scrolls. The statement in the Manual of Discipline that at the end of time God will purify man by pouring forth the spirit of truth on him is reminiscent of John's teaching that the Messiah would baptize his people with the Holy Ghost."[7]

That sounds very cautious, and Millar Burrows is tormented by the very idea that it is "not at all improbable that John knew about the ideas of the Qumran sect."[8] There is no need for anyone who has seen the barren plain that lies between the oases of Qumran and Jericho to be so circumspect.

The Viennese Orientalist Kurt Schubert wrote in his book *The Dead Sea Community:* "The place where John baptised in the Jordan, just before it flows into the Dead Sea, was not far from the monastery of Qumran, which was in its second flowering at the time. Given such a state of affairs, it is inconceivable that there was no contact between the two."

However there is not a single document that mentions John's membership in the Qumran sect, and we can only say that his connection with the Sons of Light seems possible geographically and probable through the similarities in doctrine. But in Luke, quite unexpectedly after Zacharias, John's father, utters his song of praise, in which light and darkness are mentioned, comes an observation that we now read with fresh attention: "And the child grew, and waxed strong in spirit, and was in the deserts till the day of his shewing unto Israel." There are two remarkable things here: his presentation to the people of Israel ready to start his work, as if it had been secret before, and the word "deserts." Zacharias, John's father, was a priest in the temple at Jerusalem, i.e., he was one of the froward priests. Luke's account of the remarkable episode says that Zacharias was dumb until his son's birth, that he called him John, meaning "God is merciful," although none of his kindred was called John, that he praised God in unusual language, and that then John grew up in the desert.

We know that Nicodemus, the ruler from Jerusalem (John 3), also sympathized with Rabbi J., as did Joseph of Arimathaea, the counselor, who buried him. In Josephus's account of the Essenes I find: "Scorning wedlock, they select other men's children while still pliable and teachable, and fashion them after their own pattern."

If we assume that John the Baptist was brought up at Qumran, that he summoned people to repentance and baptism (in the Essene sense) by the Jordan (as we know), that he was great enough to recognize another man as the "Lamb of God" and Messiah, one the latchet of whose shoes he was unworthy to unloose, would this Messiah have been a complete unknown who came to the Jordan by chance, perhaps even a Son of Darkness, who had not prepared the way of the Lord in the desert of Qumran? If John the Baptist, who was connected with the Essenes, recognized in Rabbi J. the Messiah for whom the way had to be prepared in the wilderness and nowhere else, should not the teaching of the Essenes be recognizable in Rabbi J.'s teaching through all the filters?

Seven

LUNAR CALENDAR
AND LAST SUPPER

Aʙᴏᴜᴛ 950 ᴀ.ᴅ., Al Qirqisani, a Jew, wrote
that there was a certain sect that hid its books in caves.
Later two Mohammedan authors refer to it, and one
of them, Al Biruni, says that these cave people, who
lived before Christ, were reputed to have had a strange
calendar. The Sabbath was not the day of rest, but the
night between the third and fourth days, i.e., the night
of our Wednesday, from which "they counted the
days and months—and the great cycle of festivals begins then, for it was on the fourth day that God created
the stars. Accordingly the Passover began on Wednesday."[1]

This way of counting is obviously based on the idea
that it did not make sense to talk about days and nights
before the stars were created on the fourth day of creation. On the other hand, the Jewish way of reckoning
the Sabbath is based on the idea that God rested on the
seventh day. Consequently the Jewish day of rest is on
Saturday—from the Christian point of view—or, more
accurately, since in the East the day is reckoned from
the onset of darkness, from Friday night to Saturday
night.

This remarkable way of reckoning the days of the
week turns up again in the so-called Damascus (or
Zadokite) Document. It was found in the synagogue

of the Jewish Karaite community in Old Cairo and gets its name from an emigration to Damascus. The document, discovered in the last century, had no parallels in Jewish literature. It mentioned a Teacher of Righteousness, a new covenant, and a froward priest.

When the Dead Sea scrolls were deciphered, scholars found the parallels. Parts of the Damascus Document were copied by the Essene monks and kept in Cave 6, although many details did not tally exactly with the teachings of the Essenes. In other words, the Damascus Document is part of the Essene library, for the strange way of reckoning the days of the week also recurs in the texts that were found by the Dead Sea.[2]

Whereas the other Jews—even today—use the lunar calendar, in which the months are shorter than in the solar calendar, it was very important for the Essenes at Qumran, "neither [to] advance the statutory times, nor [to] postpone the prescribed seasons or festivals."[3]

As proof of their conviction, the Essenes had copied out the relevant passages in the Old Testament. They were rediscovered in the caves, for example the passage from the Book of Jubilees where it says that, "there will be people who observe the moon exactly; for this corrupts the time and advances it by ten days year after year. So for them years will come when they mistake the Day of Atonement and make it an ordinary day, and an impure day into a feast day. . . . So I order thee and testify so that thou mayest testify unto them; for after thy death thy children shall act perversely by not observing a year of 364 days, and so they will confuse new moon and time and Sabbath and feast days. . . ."[4]

This observation is correct, for the extra six hours in the solar year can easily be corrected every four years by the insertion of a single day. With the lunar calendar, on the other hand, the corrections are complicated and only possible after such lengthy periods of time that in the interim whole days get displaced. The lunar calendar gains eleven days on the solar calendar in a single year, so that with the passage of time whole months have to be inserted—in order to make the spring new moon coincide with the Sabbath again, for example.

As the Essenes were especially strict about keeping the Mosaic law and the Jewish feast days, it must also have been important for them to keep the calendar as accurate as possible. A festival celebrated on the wrong day was no festival. It can be proved from the Dead Sea scrolls that the Essenes did, in fact, observe the solar calendar.

In the "War Scroll"[5] the number of fathers of the community corresponding to the number of weeks in the solar calendar is given as fifty-two and the number of major officials as twenty-six, i.e., half of fifty-two. Thus every major official would have to serve for one week twice a year, whereas the temple at Jerusalem had only twenty-four major officials in accordance with the length of the lunar year. So it can be stated with certainty: "In the temple at Jerusalem the lunar calendar was observed, among the Qumran Essenes the solar calendar. Consequently they had a feast day when the others had a weekday."[6]

But what has this got to do with Rabbi J., whose shadowy biography we are trying to illuminate? Whereabouts in the gospels is there the slightest mention of lunar and solar calendars, so that we can establish a link between him and the Dead Sea sect from another point of view? Where does it say that the Rabbi counted the days of the week from Wednesday like the Essenes, so that the Sabbath fell on a different day from that in the Jerusalem calendar?

There are two allusions to it, one direct, the other indirect. The indirect allusion is connected with the frequency with which Rabbi J. performed cures on the Sabbath, although the rule against healing on the day of rest could be broken only in cases of mortal danger, and among the Essenes, not even then.[7] If Rabbi J. did not intend to annul one jot or tittle of the law, it sounds unlikely that he would have performed forbidden actions on the Sabbath, even if it was made for man and not vice versa. This favors the interpretation that it was not a Sabbath to Rabbi J. and that according to his reckoning he was healing on a weekday, although it was a holy day to the indignant Pharisees.

Because we have no idea how strict the Sabbath law was, we do not find anything unusual about the Rabbi walking through the cornfields with his disciples on a Sabbath—in other words, taking a country walk outside the town.[8] That was quite out of the question on a Sabbath, for one of the Sabbath commandments laid down that people were allowed to circulate only within the town limits, or at the most allowed to go a thousand cubits (about fifteen hundred feet) outside them, as the Damascus Document prescribes. Here, too, it seems obvious to assume that it was not a Sabbath in the Rabbi's view, but was one according to the Pharisees' reckoning, and that they at once attacked him for that reason.

But there is also a crucial point in Rabbi J.'s life that can be explained only by the Essenes' calendar and provides a direct allusion. It is the date of the Last Supper. Millar Burrows sums up the problem as follows: "The difficulty consists in reconciling the accounts of the first three gospels with St. John's. The Passover meal was held on the night of 14th Nisan, since the day was reckoned from nightfall to nightfall. According to the synoptic gospels J.'s Last Supper was a passover meal on the night of 14th Nisan and he was crucified on 15th Nisan. In the gospel according to St. John, he was crucified on 14th Nisan. . . ."[9]

This reckoning has led some scholars to claim that the fourth evangelist had absolutely no idea of Jewish usage and customs, and that consequently he was probably not a Jew, but a Greek, or at least an author who was under Hellenistic influences, which would also tally with St. John's conspicuous anti-Semitism. If Rabbi J. wanted to celebrate the Passover meal, he could only do so on the right date, because before then there was no unleavened bread, without which the Seder night, the night of the Passover feast, could not be celebrated.

If, on the other hand, we rely on the chronology of

Matthew, Mark, and Luke, we get into difficulties with the dates, as Shalom Ben Chorin has shown: "If he is supposed to have been arrested by the Jewish authorities on this night, after the feast (i.e., on the Jerusalem temple's Sabbath), it would have been inconceivable for the trial to have taken place in the house of Caiaphas, the high priest, on this holiest of holy nights, for J. to have been handed over to Pilate on the morning of the feast, and to have been crucified on the first day of the Passover festival. Moreover the gospels keep on saying that everything had to be done quickly because of the approaching Sabbath, but never mention that the feast day would be profaned by a trial, execution, and burial.

"Anyone who is familiar with Jewish law and customs at once feels that all this is a sheer impossibility. If J. had been arrested on the Seder night, he would have been held in custody until after the feast days, and all the rest would have taken place afterward . . . the obvious inconsistency has only been solved today, for as Hermann Raschke so rightly says, 'everything is different after Qumran.' We may assume here that J., who was openly opposed to the Pharisees and Sadducees, and presumably had contacts with the Qumran sect through his rabbi, John the Baptist, used the Qumran solar calendar, so that his Seder feast took place one day earlier than that of the official priesthood in Jerusalem."[10]

If we base ourselves on the reckoning of the fourth evangelist and consequently on the Qumran calendar,

82

Rabbi J. could still have been judged, crucified, and buried before the Israelites' normal date for the Passover. Any other reckoning either disregards the strict Jewish Sabbath customs or tries to distort the true state of affairs, like the synoptic gospels, which unanimously write: ". . . on the first day of the feast of unleavened bread," and so get the reckoning wrong.

But if Rabbi J. celebrated the Seder meal (the Last Supper) before the Jerusalem Seder night, he must have had great difficulty as a stranger in obtaining not only unleavened bread, but also the necessary ritual utensils. For the law demands that on the night before the Passover feast all the everyday pots, plates, and utensils be exchanged for the kosher Passover utensils —a circumstance that even today compels every Jew and every hotel under kosher management to have entirely separate cooking and eating utensils ready for this one week and, in hotels at least, to exchange them in the presence of a rabbi.

So Rabbi J. could not simply go into the first inn he came across and order the Seder feast. The Passover utensils had not yet been brought and could not be brought, since nonkosher food was still being eaten—a fact that seems quite unimportant to a Western Christian, but is of the utmost significance to a Jew, because the *only* way in which he can express his faith is by observing the law.

Thus the premise for an earlier Seder feast based on the Qumran calendar was that in Jerusalem, too, there lived Essenes, who had already prepared everything, for only the Essenes, who celebrated their Sabbath earlier than the other Jews, could accept J. and his disciples at the Seder feast. So what we learn about in Sunday school as a miraculous prophecy by Our Lord suddenly becomes nothing more than the passing on of an Essene address. When the disciples ask where they are to prepare the Passover meal, J. answers: "Go ye into the city, and there shall meet you a man bearing a pitcher of water: follow him. And wheresoever he shall go in, say ye to the goodman of the house, The Master saith, Where is the guest-chamber, where I shall eat the passover with my disciples? And he will shew you a large upper room furnished and prepared: there make ready for us."[11]

Without reference to the Essenes this episode would be so banal that one could not help wondering why the evangelists found it worth mentioning at all. In later ages people no longer understood it and interpreted it as an example of the Rabbi's prophetic gifts. The filter of Occidental incomprehension obscured its true meaning.

Two other details also rapidly lost their meaning for non-Jewish Christians, because they did not differentiate between the various Jewish traditions.

For example we find it quite normal for Rabbi J. to have eaten the Last Supper with his twelve disciples. But according to Jewish custom—even in those days—women and members of the family partook of the meal, just as Christmas is not an exclusively male feast with us. Several passages in the New Testament tell us that

Jesus was in the company of women. Women were present at the crucifixion (according to the accounts, even his own mother); women were also the first to go to the tomb.

Why were these women not present at this important meal? Shalom Ben Chorin writes: "The fact that only the twelve disciples took part in the meal, in accordance with the Qumran rules, also suggests the influence of Qumran on J.'s last Seder in Jerusalem."[12] According to these rules, only members of the Essene group were allowed to partake of the ritual meals—and membership was confined to men.[13]

In the Manual of Discipline of the Essenes, the rule governing meals is followed by another rule: "This is the rule governing public sessions. The priests are to occupy the first place. The elders are to come second, and the rest of the people are to take their places according to their respective ranks. . . ."[14]

In connection with this, there is a passage in the New Testament where the disciples quarrel about who has precedence over the others. It comes exactly where one would expect, at the beginning of the account of the Last Supper: "And there was also a strife among them, which of them should be accounted the greatest."[15]

Even the fourth evangelist, who says nothing about a Last Supper in the sense that the synoptic gospels do, introduces the washing of feet at this point. As with the other evangelists, it serves to put a new interpretation on precedence: "If I then, your Lord and Master, have washed your feet; ye also ought to wash one another's feet. . . . Verily, verily, I say unto you, The servant is not greater than his Lord. . . ."[16]

Obviously for St. John the Seder meal took place so normally according to the rules for the feast that he does not even mention the two blessings that are usual when breaking bread and handing around the cup of wine. Breaking bread and handing around the cup of wine were and still are part and parcel of the Seder feast and, down to the individual words that are spoken on these occasions in memory of the exodus from Egypt, are nothing more than the normal unfolding of the feast that is celebrated year after year.[17] But we Western successors of a Jewish sect look on it as something special, the "institution of a sacrament." What is really strange, the different date for the Last Supper, the all-male assembly and the quarrel about seating arrangements, we accept without comment because we know no better. In reality what we take for granted is the strange thing, namely what leads back into the past behind Rabbi J., whereas we are accustomed to look on him as the beginning of the new. It is just the same with his teaching.

HERE are passages in the Bible that remain mean-
ingless even in the most accurate translation, such as
the sentence about the salt that loses its savor, that
"becomes stupid," as Luther translates it, and is cast
out.[1] Salt cannot lose its savor; if it does it is not salt.
It seems probable that J. is using a quite different kind
of simile that we no longer understand, just as the
statement that everyone shall be "salted with fire"[2] obviously comes from a world whose mental imagery was
quite different from ours.

The first beatitude from the Sermon on the Mount
in Matthew is also one of these unintelligible biblical
passages.

Luther translates it literally: "Blessed are they who
are spiritually poor, for the kingdom of heaven is
theirs."[3] A more recent German Catholic edition translates equally correctly and literally, but in the opposite
sense: "Blessed are the poor in spirit, for theirs is the
kingdom of heaven."[4]

Both versions attempt to link the word *poor* with
the word *pneuma* or *spiritus* in an intelligible way.
The result in Luther is people who are religiously
lacking; in the other, which is equally unlikely, people
who are lacking in courage. Since the beatitudes as a
whole console the underprivileged, both versions sound

right. But why was something as valuable as the kingdom of heaven promised precisely to them? Should we not assume that the first beatitude states the general theme?

But whereas all the other beatitudes are worded clearly and intelligibly, the first one remains obscure and ambiguous, so that even serious modern translations of the Bible offer increasingly fantastic interpretations that throw accuracy to the winds. The official *New English Bible* of 1961 understands the poverty financially and makes the spirit knowledge: "How blest are they who know that they are poor, the kingdom of heaven belongs to them."[5] *The NT 68—the Narratives, Letters and Testimony of the New Testament in Modern German* also puts an economic interpretation on it: "Happy are they who rejoice in being poor: the kingdom of God belongs to them!"[6] *The New Testament for Men of Our Time* (another German edition) simply does not understand the verse and says: "God loves men who beg for the spirit as beggars a gift, to them the kingdom is allotted."[7]

None of the modern translations asks whether the concept of *pauperes spiritu* has any parallels in literature or whether it has a history from which the hidden meaning could be clearly interpreted. As these parallels do exist and as we do know the history of this concept, it borders on dishonesty and deliberate suppression of the historical truth when theologians, clergymen, and biblical institutes behave as if they knew better out of conservative stubborness or Occidental arrogance.

Perhaps one has to be a Jew like Shalom Ben Chorin

to say the obvious, because, unlike the Christians, he is not abandoning any cherished but deluded ideas: "Who are the poor in spirit or the spiritually poor? Are they the intellectually retarded? Is this a glorification of simplicity, naïveté, or even stupidity? Is this verse a consolation for the uneducated as opposed to the haughty scribes?" That might be a more feasible assumption, but a glance at the Dead Sea scrolls gives a different and more reliable answer. Here, in the Qumran sect, we learn about the concept of *aniye haruach*, those who remained poor for the spirit's sake. These are the people who put into practice the Franciscan ideal of poverty centuries before Francis of Assisi, who renounced worldly possessions so as to be able to devote themselves entirely to the spirit.

It becomes clear from J.'s parables that he shared the Qumran sect's contempt for earthly goods. "For what is a man profited, if he shall gain the whole world, and lose his own soul?" (Matthew 16:26.) "It is easier for a camel to go through the eye of a needle, than for a rich man to enter the kingdom of God." (Matthew 19:24.) "Lay not up for yourselves treasures upon earth, where moth and rust doth corrupt . . . but lay up for yourselves treasures in heaven." (Matthew 6:19–20.)

It would be possible to quote many of J.'s words, or words attributed to him, which express the same idea. The spiritually poor, with whose beatitude the Sermon on the Mount begins, are, then, those who remained poor deliberately in order to prepare themselves for the spirit, the spirit of God, in the knowledge that all kinds of sin shall be forgiven except the sin against the Holy Ghost (Matthew 12:31).[9]

Kurt Schubert of the Viennese Institute for Judaism confirms this in his book *The Dead Sea Community:* "The man who is poor in spirit is neither a pauper nor a fool. The same conception of poor is also found in the Qumran texts. The community called itself a community of the poor, and the members called themselves poor for the sake of the spirit, poor in the expectation of grace, and poor in expectation of thy (i.e., God's) salvation."[10]

And even Millar Burrows, professor at Yale University, who has written several hundred pages trying to show the differences between Christianity and Qumran, has to admit that "Many of the contacts between J.'s sayings and the Dead Sea scrolls are in the area of moral teaching. Especially striking are the parallels in the Sermon on the Mount. . . . There is a text from the Cave 4 containing a series of beatitudes beginning with the word 'blessed,' like those of Matthew 5:3 ff."[11]

In this way the celebrated beatitudes of the Sermon on the Mount, which many look on as the epitome of Christian consolation, regain their real meaning. Like the parables with their concealed meaning, like the allusions to the Sons of Light and of Darkness, like the date of the Last Supper, the beatitudes can be understood only in their original sense when seen from the Qumran point of view. They, too, are codes for the initiate, not glad tidings for everyone.

The kingdom of heaven was not a universal prize for everyone; it was reserved for the Essenes, the people who professed the true faith, who introduced communal property and renounced riches, who kept the 613 commandments and prohibitions of the Mosaic law, who observed the rites of purification and kept the secrets of the new covenant.

That and nothing else is the meaning of the first beatitude. Any other interpretation contradicts what J. meant and said here, however Christian it may sound to our ears. What matters is not what theologians have made out of it for two millennia, but what was actually meant. The other six beatitudes do not introduce anything that had not already been mentioned by Josephus and Philo as characteristic of the Essenes, and the phrase about those who hunger and thirst after righteousness and the consolation for those who are persecuted for the sake of righteousness at once evoke the memory of the "Teacher of Righteousness" whom the Essene community revered.

It may be just coincidence that the passage about the light of the world comes immediately after the beatitudes in Matthew, and that the "Sons of Light" recur over and over again in the scrolls. It may also be a coincidence that Matthew then adds the passage in which Rabbi J., in the Essene manner, intensifies the law of Moses with his "But I say unto you," rather than transcends it, as we in the West think. But I claim that even the skeptic can no longer call it a coincidence when the next verse says that swearing is forbidden (as it was by the Essenes but not by other Jews) and is followed shortly afterward by a prayer that is directly in line with the apocalyptic expectation of the end of the world and in which it says: "Thy kingdom come. Thy will be done in earth as it is in heaven."[12]

The wisdom of a monastic community by the Dead Sea that wanted to hasten the kingdom of heaven on earth by leading lives pleasing to God; not supersession of the Mosaic law, but its unconditional intensification to include mental sin; codes for the initiate—that is the core of Rabbi J.'s teaching, firmly embedded in the cosmic framework of the coming dominion of God on earth which meant hope in this world, verifiable and real, announced by the coming of the Messiah, the savior from oppressors and foreign powers and religions, but no hope in the other world. For that is the meaning of the Jewish Apocalypse: to recognize the sign when God the Father shall set up his heavenly kingdom on earth, so that people can do penance in time.

That is what John the Baptist summoned people to —for the kingdom of heaven was at hand—that is the point of such parables as the wise and foolish virgins who await the bridegroom, and that is why we find the apocalyptic descriptions in the New Testament: coded messages for the initiate.

For out of the bewildering wealth of apocalyptic ideas we find only certain specific ones in the New Testament, for example in the twenty-fourth chapter of St. Matthew. There it says as the acme of horror that many false prophets shall arise and that unbelief shall prevail before the inconceivable happens: "When ye therefore shall see the abomination of desolation, spoken of by Daniel the prophet, stand in the holy place (whoso readeth, let him understand), Then let them which be in Judaea flee into the mountains."[13]

If we refer to Daniel we read: "And arms shall stand on his part, and they shall pollute the sanctuary of strength and shall take away the daily sacrifice, and they shall place the abomination of desolation that maketh desolate."[14]

The author of Daniel was a contemporary of the Maccabees and obviously refers to a topical event, which he sets in the future to make himself look like a prophet. If we consult Maccabees, we find the exact description of this "abomination."[15] In those days, about 180 B.C., King Antiochus IV, one of the Greek Diadochi, had plundered the temple in Jerusalem and desecrated it by installing a statue of Zeus. At the time it was this abomination that drove the Chasidim, the pious, out into the wilderness to await the end of the world, for the very worst had happened to their sanctuary.

Now Rabbi J. need not have referred to this particular example. In his day there were all kinds of expectations of the end of the world, and Daniel was not one of the prophets recognized by Judaism. If in spite of that this specific example was introduced, combined with the secretive wording of the parable—whoso readeth, let him understand, he that hath ears to hear, let him hear—then there must have been a hidden meaning behind the obvious one, a meaning which an Essene understood at once. For the desecration of the temple by Antiochus IV, which had led in the past to the founding of the desert sect of Qumran, became once again two hundred years later a coded warning to the initiate, which was to come true in tragic fashion when the temple was destroyed in the year 70 and the Jewish people were scattered to the four winds.

The memory of the abomination of Antiochus was a warning and a sign of the imminent coming of the Messiah and God's kingdom, i.e., the God-given dominion of the Jews over the world that had hitherto oppressed them. Babylonian captivity, dominion of the Greeks, and occupation by the Romans—all that had to be compensated for among the "chosen people" by hope in this world, if Yahweh existed at all. The servant of God, whom Isaiah in Babylon had dreamed of as a liberator, became the savior, the Messiah of the present. And the same kind of sacrilege that had once driven the Essenes to withdraw into the caves by the Dead Sea, would now two hundred years later be repeated by the Romans. They, too, would desecrate the Temple and Yahweh would not leave his people in the lurch this time, any more than in the past when the Maccabees triumphed briefly over the Greeks. What the people of Qumran had hoped for two hundred years was preached once again by Rabbi J. in his day and for his day.

Sermon on the Mount and Apocalypse, repentance and baptism, communal property and poverty, Last Supper and new covenant, can all be found again in this constellation and form only in the Qumran scrolls. What we have looked on as the teaching of Rabbi J. for nearly two thousand years was written down before his birth. Thus Frank Moore Cross, one of the scholars who deciphered the scrolls, comes to the conclusion: "At all events we are now in a position to use Qumran discoveries to lend weight to the view that the Testaments are indeed Judeo-Christian editions, in part reworked, of old Essene sources."[16] "The direct use of Essene or proto-Essene materials in Christian compositions, and, indeed, the publication of Christian compilations of Essene or proto-Essene sources can now be documented impressively."[17] "We must now affirm that in the Essene communities we discover antecedents of Christian forms and concepts."[18]

And even in the passage in Luke where the angels announce at Christmas: "Glory to God in the highest and on earth peace to men of good will"[19]—even there Qumran, the Essene settlement by the Dead Sea, emerges again in the background. Over and over again the sons and the men of good will are mentioned in the Qumran scrolls—and nowhere else. They are the "poor in spirit" in whom God is well pleased.[20]

An unbroken chain of references to the Essene community by the Dead Sea runs from Rabbi J.'s baptism, on through his teaching, and down to the Last Supper. That being so, how could people so misunderstand J., the sectarian, as to make him the founder of a new universal religion, when all he wanted was to reconcile the chosen people, his people, the Jews, with Yahweh, because the kingdom of God was at hand? Who made an itinerant Jewish preacher and prophet into the founder of a universal religion that finally clashed with Judaism? What is the filter that obscured everything?

Nine

THE REASON
FOR THE SILENCE

IF we read the New Testament without knowing the accounts of Josephus, Philo, and the Dead Sea scrolls, it would never occur to us that a sect like the Essenes existed side by side with the Pharisees and Sadducees. Comparison with the scrolls, which were older, first showed the New Testament's dependence on Qumran, and the Essene library first enabled us to decipher the message which was deliberately concealed in the parables: "By hearing ye shall hear and shall not understand; and seeing ye shall see, and shall not perceive. . . . But blessed are your eyes, for they see: and your ears, for they hear."[1]

In its zeal Christianity at once identified itself with the disciples and claimed that it had correctly understood and reproduced the message.

The error is understandable, for the gospels did everything they could to obscure the historical connections in J.'s life. For them Rabbi J. emerges from anonymity, accepts his ministry at his baptism, teaches, is persecuted and put to death. A comet that follows its course and burns itself out.

The question is, Why did this obscuring process take place? The mere fact that the Essenes had a secret doctrine cannot be the reason for not even admitting their existence, for John the Baptist and the Rabbi appeared publicly, and Josephus described the Essenes in detail.

So it is difficult to see why the writers of the New Testament kept their narratives about Rabbi J. so free of points of reference, especially because at the end they cannot explain how such a peace-loving and devout man could be executed on a political charge, in the company of thieves and murderers, by the Roman occupying power. Admittedly the motive is mentioned in the gospels, namely his claim to be the Messiah—the religious and political savior of the people. But at no point in the gospels is there any preparatory treatment of this motive. There is no mention of political activity; there is no call to rebellion. On the contrary, when the Rabbi was asked the question about taxes, a question intended to sound him about the possibility of opposition to the Roman occupying power, he answered diplomatically: "Render therefore unto Caesar the things which are Caesar's; and unto God the things that are God's."[2]

A statesmanlike answer that we find quite in order. Consequently we do not ask how Herod's followers ever came to ask the Rabbi this question, if he wandered about the country so peacefully and had only the spiritual welfare of his Jewish fellow citizens at heart. Yet there must have been at least a suspicion that Rabbi J. or his disciples had some connection with an uprising against the Romans. The fact that he was hailed by the masses on his entry into Jerusalem as the Messiah and that he saw himself as Christ, the anointed one, is described clearly and unambiguously by the evangelists. So the Messianic role itself could scarcely have been the reason for obscuring what had happened and making it appear to have no historical connections. Lastly, Rabbi J.'s disciples called themselves Christians, i.e., Messianists, followers of the Messiah.

But obviously there must have been something that alerted the Romans and that the evangelists subsequently tried to hush up. Obviously Rabbi J. was more than a mere prophet.

Since the administration of religious and civil justice was in the hands of the Jews, actual revolt and resistance must have existed from the Romans' point of view before they intervened. So let us assume that Rabbi J. or his disciples had had some connection with revolt against the Roman government.

We now know that there was such an organized resistance among the Jews—the only thing is that we cannot connect Rabbi J. with it from the Bible. Once again it was Josephus who wrote about these resistance fighters, the so-called Zealots, who went on fighting even after the destruction of Jerusalem and defended the mountain fortress of Massada on the Dead Sea against the Romans for three years, until they killed themselves just before its conquest rather than fall into the hands of the hated enemy.

The Zealots are also mentioned several times in the Bible, but the reader often finds them described in terms which emphasize their piety and seem to lack any political overtones—not without reason, it appears. Joel Carmichael writes on this subject: "Today the

Zealots would be called diehards or irreconcilables. They were extremists who refused to accept the rule of Rome or her vassals. The word 'Zealot' itself applies to one who was zealous for the Law; it was taken from a celebrated passage in one of the Old Testament Apocrypha, *I Maccabees* 2:27–31: 'And Matthew cried out in the city with a loud voice, saying "Whosoever is zealous for the Law and maintains the covenant, let him come forth after me." Then many that sought after justice and judgment went down into the wilderness to dwell there.' "[3]

This quotation from the First Book of Maccabees is the foundation charter, so to speak, of the Essenes. It is this passage that tells us that the Chasidim, the devout, went into the desert and lived in caves because they could no longer tolerate the godlessness of their time (*cf* Chapter 5).

As so often in Israel's history the themes of faith and politics were inseparably bound up. The fight for the law of Moses also meant a fight against the foreign occupiers and their sacrilegious religions. In the time of the Maccabees it was the Greeks, around the birth of Christ it was the Romans.

The man who was zealous in the faith was always a Zealot against the foreigner, too, whom he actually experienced in history as an occupying power. The truly devout man was intrinsically also the true rebel, whether he took up a sword or not. So it is not surprising that one of the most important documents discovered in the Qumran caves is the so-called War Scroll, in which the War of the Sons of Light and the

Sons of Darkness is described in technical terms based on Roman patterns of military organization that would delight a military historian.

The idea that the Essenes were at least partly Zealots, i.e., radical extremists, contradicts everything that we know about them to date. Josephus and Philo expressly describe the sect as peaceful and quite uninterested in politics, as would be natural with men living in an uninhabited desert. It was precisely the marked love of peace in those turbulent days that had already aroused astonishment at the amazing similarity between the Essenes' doctrine and the teaching of Rabbi J. in the New Testament.

It is strange how sometimes discoveries can remain as it were "in the family." The Jewish archeologist Sukenik was one of the first to hear about the discoveries of the scrolls by the Dead Sea, and it was his son, Yigael Yadin, when he was in the United States, who managed to buy back for the Jewish people the same Isaiah scroll that his father had almost acquired in Jerusalem. It was the same Yigael Yadin who excavated Massada, the last stronghold of the Zealots by the Dead Sea, from 1963 to 1965 and found there, to his astonishment, among the debris of two thousand years, writings of the supposedly peaceful Essenes of Qumran.

"I came across the lines 'Song of the sixth Sabbath sacrifice on the ninth of the second month.' This and a few other lines showed that the text tallied with a document from Cave 4 at Qumran. In other words it was the scroll of a sect, in which the 'Songs of the Sabbath sacrifice' were written down in detail, with each Sabbath being given a date.

"But the sixth Sabbath could only fall on the ninth of the second month if we assume that a particular sect, namely the Qumran sect, was involved. In fact the document we had found was written by that sect. In its calendar the year was divided into 364 days . . . the first day of the first month, i.e., the month of Nisan, always fell on a Wednesday, the day when the stars were created, which entailed the division of time. . . ."[5]

The Essenes' solar calendar, according to which Rabbi J. celebrated his Passover meal on a different day from the other Jews, is the connecting link. Were the Essenes Zealots, or the Zealots Essenes? Yigael Yadin asks: "How did a scroll of this sect reach Massada? . . . It seems to me that the scroll proves the participation of the Essenes in the revolt against the Romans. . . . In addition, the works of Josephus contain a direct reference to Essene participation in the war. When he enumerates the instigators of the revolt and names the districts under their command, he writes that the commanding officer of the important central district was a certain 'John the Essene.' Is it probable that only a single Essene supported the revolt and at the same time was appointed to an important command? That seems quite out of the question. It is far more likely that a large number of Essenes took part in the uprising and withdrew with their comrades in arms to the last remaining stronghold of Massada. . . . That in my view is the explanation of the find of the Qumran scroll at Massada."[6]

The idea that the message of peace and love should have originated among political resistance fighters is unfamiliar to say the least. But why not? Fundamentally the Zealots ended as they began—in battle against the "heathen" and their religions. Yigael Yadin draws the following conclusions: "For some reason or other we have been handed down a distorted picture of the Essenes that largely springs from Philo's account; for scholars have tried to deduce from his description that the Essenes were pacifists, in the modern sense of the word. I find this thesis untenable. It was only in wars that ran counter to their beliefs, i.e., wars not willed by God, that they did not take part. But if we assume that they were convinced that the great rebellion meant the God-ordained war against the Romans, then there was absolutely no reason for them to abstain from it."[7] When the Qumran monastery was excavated, arrowheads for defensive and offensive use were found.

But Rabbi J. died thirty years before the fall of Massada, and Christian sensibility can feel secure again. Of course Yigael Yadin thinks that the discovery of the Massada scroll will occupy scholars more than all the other finds and be the subject of stormy arguments among experts[8]—but years will pass before this archeological achievement penetrates the consciousness of the theologians, if indeed they ever feel interested, because inconvenient truths ought not to exist. Basically the Massada find is only a confirmation of what is in the New Testament in any case. It is simply not true that Rabbi J. was surrounded by harmless devout disciples who were so naïve that they did not even understand the parables and tramped through the cornfields with fluttering beards. There is every indication that at least six of the twelve disciples were Zealots, that is to say resistance fighters.

Luke's list of apostles openly introduces Simon as "Simon called Zelotes," an appellation that in the past sounded quite as harmless to us as that of the other disciple "Simon, named Peter." The second name of yet another disciple is less harmless than was once assumed, for what was previously taken as a place name really means membership in a radical branch of the Zealots, the Sicarii, or dagger-men. The Hebrew-Aramaic method of writing, which consists solely of consonants and omits the vowels, wrote the Latin word as Iskariot, or as we know the name: Iscariot. Even an otherwise conservative biblical lexicon states that Judas Iscariot, the betrayer, whose nickname should be translated as "dagger-man," was probably a member of the party of Zealots.

Simon Peter, whose first act when the Rabbi was taken prisoner was to seize a sword, may also have been a Zealot. In Matthew the Rabbi calls him "Simon Barjona,"[11] which is normally translated as "Simon, son of Jona," for Bar means son. It is the passage where Rabbi J. says to Peter: "Thou art Peter, and upon this rock will I build my church"—and we are entitled to ask why Peter is suddenly described as the son of Jona at this crucial moment. But here the same thing has happened as with Judas. What in the one case was misunderstood as his place of origin (from Scariot) was misinterpreted in Peter's case as denoting a relationship. Bar-jona is an

Aramaic word and can equally well be read as "open land." Those who lived outside the city were, in the plural form of Bar-jona, the Baryonim. Joel Carmichael states: "Now, the famous proto-Zealot . . . , Judas the Galilean, is occasionally referred to as a 'man living on the outside.' This curious phrase is clarified by another remark, in the Talmud, about a nephew of the famous Rabbi Yohanan ben Zakkai who was called the 'dagger-man,' and was the head of the *baryonim* of Jerusalem.

"The word *baryonim* comes from an Aramaic word meaning open country; they were those people living in the open country outside the towns, that is, the outcasts, outlaws, and extremists that the country was full of. Paul himself was mistaken for such a daggerman by a Roman captain of a cohort: 'Are you not the Egyptian . . . who recently stirred up a revolt and led the four thousand daggermen out into the wilderness?' (*Acts* 21-38).

"It is plain from the context that the *baryonim* were similar in all respects to the Zealots."[12]

So Rabbi J. did not make some nondescript son of Jona the "cornerstone" of the church, but one of the Baryonim, a man who according to St. John was a disciple of John the Baptist by the Dead Sea, a militant Essene from the desert in which the people of Qumran awaited the fulfillment of the new covenant. On thee, the outcast, will I build my church—would anyone say that, or would it be attributed to him, unless he was a Baryona himself?

Thus three disciples—Simon the Zealot, Simon Peter

the Baryona, and Judas the dagger-man—are clearly labeled. If we now read through the list of apostles again, we find that two more disciples, James and John, the sons of Zebedee, were called "Boanerges," the sons of thunder. Unless this was intended to describe their turbulent natures, something that would have suited Peter much better, it is very likely that their nickname too had some connection with the Zealots. And strangely enough James was executed later, just like other rebels.

Lastly, as we read in the gospel according to St. John, Simon Peter the Baryona had yet another brother called Andrew, who was one of the Rabbi's first disciples. How could Andrew have helped being a Zealot, if his brother Simon Peter was one?

In other words, it is possible that half the disciples were Zealots—grounds enough for the Roman occupation forces to take an interest in this group that had formed around Rabbi J. The Rabbi answered the question about tribute money loyally: render unto Caesar the things that are Caesar's. He was either opposed to some of his disciples or lying, or the saying was not his at all. Mystery or falsification?

But who could have been interested in making the movement seem harmless and misrepresenting its meaning? The archeologist Yigael Yadin has stated that for some reason or other a distorted picture of the Essenes has been handed down. Who touched up the picture—and why?

HE title Christ is simply the Greek translation of the Hebrew word Messiah and means "the anointed one" in both languages. Kings were anointed; it was the mark of their office.

In the Old Testament tradition, the Messiah was the savior of the people of Israel. In those days that really meant that the Messiah would be the liberator from Roman rule and King of Israel. (That was why it was important that he came from the royal house of David.)

That and that alone is the meaning of the inscription on the cross, which was put there by the Romans: HIC EST J.—REX JUDAEORUM—This is J., the King of the Jews.[1]

This did not mean a religious kingship—the Romans would not have taken any action against one—but actual sovereignty over the Jewish people. It makes no difference as regards his death sentence whether Rabbi J. aspired to be king or not, whether he was a member of the Zealot resistance against the Romans or not. The fact remains that he was looked on as a political rebel and executed by the Romans on that charge.

His disciples had had to come to terms with this truth. The fact that they all fled after their master's arrest or betrayed him, like Peter, shows that they knew perfectly well how dangerous the situation was for them. James, one of the sons of thunder, was later taken prisoner and executed; Peter was imprisoned several times and finally put to death in Rome, like Paul.

The disciples' position was difficult. They were under suspicion and we can understand their trying their hardest to save their own lives by toning down or covering up every factual or suspected rebellious activity.

How this was done during the first decades after Rabbi J.'s death, we do not know. We have no firsthand witnesses from that period. The first accounts of the lives of Rabbi J. and his disciples were not written down until after the destruction of Jerusalem in the year 70. So they are at least forty years distant from the events at a time when the Jewish resistance was definitively broken and Rome held undisputed sway over its empire Longing for the coming of God's kingdom was still alive, but must have seemed unreal after the destruction of the temple and the dispersal of the Jews. A new earth on heaven grew out of the kingdom of God on earth. The apocalyptic expectation of the end had deceived; neither Rabbi J. nor another Messiah had brought liberation.

People began to idealize Rabbi J.'s life and project its actual effect into the future. The victorious "at some time" grew out of the "now" that had failed. Hand in hand with this process of idealization, which was increasingly able to dispense with the historical background because the future, not the past, was important, the filter began to obscure the scene.

It let through only those things that seemed opportune and right to the evangelists a generation after the events. The gospels do not reproduce historical truth;

they are apologias conditioned by and dependent on their time, a fact the theologians gloss over by talking about the creative influence of the early church.[2]

The gospels that we know today are not the first written evidence, but edited versions of older documents, as Luke's narrative tells us: "Forasmuch as many have taken in hand to set forth in order a declaration of those things which are most surely believed among us, Even as they delivered them unto us, which from the beginning were eye-witnesses, and ministers of the word; It seemed good to me also, having perfect understanding of all things from the very first. . . ."[3]

Thus three similar accounts, whose traditional authors are Matthew, Mark, and Luke, the synoptic evangelists, came from one original source that has not reached us. The fourth, the gospel according to St. John, on the other hand, obviously stems from a completely different source and tradition. In spite of these different original sources, the same filter effect, i.e., the same tendency on the part of the authors, can be observed in all four narratives. Everything that is Essene teaching survives their editing more or less undamaged, although its source is not acknowledged (every reference to the Essenes themselves being cut out). It is the part of the gospels which comes through the filter as "right" and which is harmless for J.'s followers. Everything that was or might appear politically dangerous, i.e., everything that did not seem opportune at a time when the Rabbi's adherents began to spread out through the Roman Empire, had to be obscured and filtered out. The process met with very little opposition because the majority of J.'s followers were no longer Jews. The political importance of Jewish Messiahhood found no echo among them and so could be replaced by the religious aspect of Messiahhood. All superfluous references to a rebel role would have been politically inept and unnecessary among the new Christians outside Judaism. They could and had to be omitted.

However, the Jews' incredible and literally maniacal fidelity to the written word saw to it that some of the references were not filtered out. Thus, just as in Mark and Matthew two contradictory versions of the feeding of the four and five thousand are left standing side by side, instead of one being rejected, the writers of the gospels did not succeed in completely altering what had once been written. They do not mention Zealots by name, but they describe them. Nowhere do we find a summons to revolt, but the passage where Rabbi J. says that he has come not to send peace but a sword is retained, because the sentence was placed in a context that permitted another interpretation. And for centuries people promptly understood the passage as saying that the sword meant the discord that arises through the acceptance or rejection of Rabbi J.'s teaching.

Another sentence was also allowed to stand, embedded in a prophecy: "But now, he that hath a purse, let him take it, and likewise his scrip: and he that hath no sword, let him sell his garment and buy one."[5]

Without directly suppressing them, the authors were able to retain old sources by putting them into new contexts. The fact that Peter cut off Malchus's ear with a sword and so confirmed a factual state of resistance against the Roman occupying power was not suppressed, but combined with another event and so rendered harmless. Rabbi J. performs a miracle and the ear is sound again. The political offense becomes a mere bagatelle; it is simply changed into the motive for an impressive feat of healing.

Naturally enough, this technique of placing sentences in altered contexts gave rise to a series of insoluble contradictions. Obviously the synoptic evangelists did not consider it opportune for Rabbi J. to have found his first disciples so close to Qumran among those extremists, the Baryonim, as John tells it. They simply transferred the story to the idyllic Lake Genesareth— and the contradiction is as complete as J.'s epiphanies in different places after his death are. Even the story of the Passion is depicted quite inconsistently in the passages that handle the relationship between Jews and Romans.

Matthew and Mark, the earliest authors, speak of "Simon of Cana" in the list of apostles; Luke, the furthest away in time from the events, can already permit himself to introduce the same Simon of Cana as "Simon, called Zelotes." Clearly in Luke's day the word Zealot was no longer as dangerous as Simon of Cana, which had the secret meaning of Zealot in Matthew and Mark's day.

Matthew and Mark only admit the connection with the extremists in a single passage, and it contains a lesson for us. Naturally it had to be Judas, the Sicarian, the dagger-man, who betrayed the Rabbi so disgracefully. There was no better way of setting themselves apart from the Zealots, and in another passage Luther actually translates the word dagger-men by assassins.

The evangelists are interpreters, not biographers; they did not illuminate events that had become dark owing to the generation gap—if anything, they darkened what still seemed too light. They did not write history; they invented it. They did not want to tell a straightforward narrative, but to justify. But everything is different since Qumran. Since the discovery of the Dead Sea scrolls, we know that what we thought of as an unavoidable blind spot was nothing but an obscuring filter whose method of operation we now understand.

Of course, once we have found a new angle from which to investigate the strange history of Rabbi J., it is easy to find more and more passages and "proofs" of our thesis, but any attempt to produce a water-tight case is bound to collapse. The whole thing is not a logical problem that works out with no remainder. Too many people and too many unknown circumstances have contributed to certain factors and facts being filtered out and changed, and it would be foolish to expect the story to work out like a game of patience, when it cannot possibly work out.

The borderline between what one man looks on as "proof" and another as stubborn adherence to wrong ideas is fluid. Yet anyone who is ready to attempt an explanation of Rabbi J.'s secret after reading the foregoing will certainly find it in the retouching of the evangelists.

The reason for the distorted picture of the Essenes that has been handed down lies in the attempt to separate the Jewish political components from the doctrine and expectation of salvation of the Essenes and so make the movement acceptable to the Romans. Since the discoveries at Massada and Qumran we know that the picture of the Essenes given by Josephus writing in the service of the Romans and Philo of Alexandria living in the Roman Empire is not accurate.

Without these Dead Sea discoveries, there would still be no point of departure or possibility of transforming the vague feeling of a mystery into scientific knowledge.

But what does the picture look like without the retouching? Authors like Schonfield and Carmichael oppose a blatantly and exclusively political interpretation to the spiritual and devout one of the West. They work from the assumption that the gospels always meant exactly the opposite of what they said. I feel that salvation and rebellion are not the only possible alternatives. Human life is not so stereotyped as we sometimes like to pretend for simplicity's sake, especially when the person concerned can no longer defend himself.

What is too simple about the Western picture of Christ to be true applies vice versa to the opposite thesis. One side has selected the purely religious aspect of a Jewish religious-cum-political phenomenon, the other solely the political. To the former the Messiah was the son of God, to the latter a failed politician. In reality he was both.

But from the passages where the evangelists cautiously concealed things and deliberately deviated from reality, Western theologians in their ignorance made a mystery that led further and further away from the man J. to a theology to which the absurd seemed credible. Relation to reality became unimportant; doctrine became the only vital criterion.

They did not ask where the doctrine came from, but what it meant—in a vacuum, so to speak. In the process they overlooked the fact that the significance of a doctrine depends entirely on the soil from which it grew. In principle Western Christianity could manage without the Old Testament and without Judaism, in spite of protestations to the contrary. Palestine and the Jews were simply the fortuitous historical background chosen by God for his intervention, and formerly there was no lack of German theologians who tried to show that Rabbi J. was an Aryan.

The scholars who thought that they recognized the "historical J." in the New Testament and, following the slogan "the Bible is right after all," constantly found their idea of him confirmed must begin to doubt whether the Bible is really so right after the finds at Qumran and Massada.

Now we know that the doctrine of Rabbi J. is not just vaguely connected with the Jewish Apocalypse and expectation of the end; we know exactly where it came from and consequently what was really meant by it—not what was read into it later. The link with Qumran and the Essenes changes the meaning of Christian doctrine. It leads back from the breadth given it by St. Paul against Rabbi J.'s intentions to the narrowness of Jewish thought, and remains there, in defiance of all later interpretations, as the only one meant by Rabbi J.

Now we know that the Jew J. had no teaching of his own, but propagated an already existing doctrine exclusively to the Jews, a doctrine that is so deeply rooted in the tradition of the Jewish people that any shifting of emphasis away from Judaism automatically implies a falsification of the original meaning.

Now we know that Rabbi J. did not have only peaceful ideas; he also—voluntarily or compulsorily—lived out the political aspect of Messiahship to its bitter end and failure. Both his followers outside Judaism to whom Jewish political Messianism meant nothing, and his disappointed Jewish adherents, who did not call themselves after Rabbi J. or his teaching, but "Christians" ("anointed ones") after his Messianic function that had failed in reality, were understandably ready to elevate reality into the ideal and make the suffering Messiah out of the savior of the people of Israel. They no longer saw Rabbi J.'s sufferings as the end of their hope, but as the beginning; those who had suffered themselves after the destruction of Jerusalem saw in him the reflection of their own situation. Because they were forced to reduce the dual meaning of Messiahship to the purely religious aspect—partly because of the Romans and partly because otherwise they could make no sense out of the life and failure of Rabbi J.—they began to put a new interpretation on the life of the Jew J. and so to falsify it.

As we can confirm today, such a shift of emphasis took place with the evangelists. They described a different Rabbi J. from the one who can now be identified by historical reality. In his book *It began with J. of*

Nazareth, Heinz Zahrnt points out the consequences of this: ". . . if historical research could prove that an irreconcilable antithesis existed between the historical J. and Christ as preached, and therefore that belief in J. has no support in J. himself, that would not only be absolutely fatal theologically, as N. A. Dahl says, but would also mean the end of all Christology. Yet I am convinced that even then we theologians would be able to find a way out—was there ever a time when we couldn't?—but we are either lying now or would be lying then."[6]

I have an answer to that quotation. But so far I have only tried to penetrate the first of the two filters that obscured the actual life of Rabbi J. I have not yet scrutinized the second filter that further distorted this darkened and mystery-enshrouded life.

Eleven

THE SECOND FILTER

THE first filter that obscured Rabbi J.'s life was used to ensure that the growing membership of the Essene Christians continued into the second generation without political taint after the catastrophical events of the year 70. It was a deliberate defense measure in order to conceal historical connections. The secret doctrine of the Essenes and the connection with Zealotism and political Messianism looked on as fatal after the year 70 made it necessary—and in the fourth gospel the filter even went so far as to blame the Jews themselves for the death of the Jew J., and not the Romans.

Since the Dead Sea finds, we have the corrective filter with which we can reilluminate the actual point of departure for Rabbi J.'s doctrine and life. We know now the religious background Rabbi J. came from and what the original—and therefore the real—meaning of his teaching was.

With this corrective filter we can solve all those mysteries in Rabbi J.'s life that characterize his spiritual origin, his teaching, and his conduct. Comparison of two-thousand-year-old documents enables us to state with considerable certainty that the teaching and claims of Rabbi J. were stamped by the Qumran Essenes—regardless of whether he was an Essene monk or had some form of close contact with the Qumran sect over a long period.

If this connection is as clear as I believe, one may naturally wonder why theological scholars did not see and admit it long ago. After all, no one can claim that "modern" theology shows any particular restraint when it comes to demolishing old, long-accepted ideas. On the contrary, it has a growing tendency to reduce everything either to myths explicable on a religious or psychological basis or to plain historical facts, not to mention the theory (formerly applied to every famous man, including Shakespeare) that J. did not exist at all.[1] So we should have expected theology to be only too glad to anchor the phenomenon of Rabbi J. in the explicable, thankful to have reached a safe haven in the flood of allegorical and symbolical interpretations.

Strangely enough the opposite is the case. Since the Enlightenment, which in its time certainly made a lot of dull and stupid statements, but also made many true predictions, theology has continually striven to argue from a plane that disregarded the state of contemporary knowledge. For example, the Herder Verlag's *Praktisches Bibellexicon* still claims, twenty-two years after the discovery of the Dead Sea scrolls, "that a significant comparison of the Qumran scriptures with the New Testament cannot be carried out until Qumran scholarship is more advanced."[2] What are we still waiting for after twenty-two years? Theology is a valid target for Edmund Wilson's reproach that a scholar in the service of the church is hindered by his religious mission from drawing the logical conclusions from the Dead Sea scrolls.[3]

There is a good deal of truth in that, for no one likes

to see himself doubted, especially when the Bible itself offers him suitable counterarguments. Thus, to name only one of many examples, the Christian-Jewish encyclopaedia *The Bible and its World*[4] writes in its chapter on Qumran and Christianity: "Both in Qumran and the New Testament the prophetical concept of a new covenant fertilized the theological self-awareness of the community. Nevertheless, even here there is a fundamental difference. In the Qumran new covenant the Law of Sinai remains the basis of the relationship with God . . . in the New Testament version a covenant was concluded through the blood of Jesus that frees from the law and fulfils the promises of God that were given even before the law."

That is right and at the same time it is wrong. It is right because that does appear in the New Testament, but it is wrong because two stages of development have been equated and compared. Naturally we find "fundamental differences" between Qumran and present-day Christianity if we ignore the fact that Rabbi J.'s teaching was further developed even during the first century of its existence. So the question is simply whether or not this further development took place in line with Rabbi J.'s original ideas or not. If we go by the words traditionally handed down as Rabbi J.'s, he did not want to alter the Law of Sinai by one jot or tittle, but on the contrary to strengthen it as a prerequisite for the new covenant.

Pauline Christianity, on the other hand, freed itself from the Jewish Mosaic law and preached the conquest of the law and redemption through Christ. Even though

we have become accustomed to consider the New Testament as a compilation of twenty-seven scriptures on the
same theme, Paul's teaching marks a break. Theology
has known this for a long time, and comparing Pauline
Christianity with Qumran is an even less admissible
procedure for that reason.

Between the traditional material of the gospels and
the teaching of St. Paul lies the tragic death of the
Messiah J. (which the disciples did not understand),
the destruction of Jerusalem and with it the collapse
of all hopes for the imminently awaited coming of the
kingdom of God on earth. What lies between the death
of the Jew J. and the epistles of St. Paul is the second
filter, which began to work simultaneously with, but
independently of, the first filter.

The second filter was not used to conceal, but rather
to try to understand and explain Rabbi J.'s life after his
death. One filter obscured historical and biographical
references; the other, working from a specific angle,
began to enlarge J.'s life, which was still visible but had
lost its connections with time and place.

The first filter was like a dark glass through which
we no longer perceive shadings and subtleties, but only
the vividly painted parts of the picture, without being
able to realize the connection between the visible parts.

The second filter worked on a different principle. It
was not a color filter like the first one, but a polarized
magnifying glass. But enlargement is not a filter per se.
Enlargement simply has the effect of making the object
observed become larger the farther away from it one

holds the glass, but from a certain point onward making it vaguer, and finally turning it upside down. The actual filter effect consists in the polarization, i.e. in the fact that there are glasses which only let the light through from one particular direction and suppress all other rays, without obscuring the picture. If you look at a shop window with polarized glasses you only perceive what lies behind it. You can no longer see the shop window and what is reflected in it. Polarization filters are invisible blinkers because they do not seem to narrow the field of vision, although you only see a fraction of what you would see normally. Any motorist who has used glasses with polarized lenses against dazzle can confirm this.

So if we assume that the apostle Paul used such polarized magnifying glasses—unlike the evangelists who only wore sunglasses tinted with one color—then we must prove it or at least make it probable. We must show where the break between the first and the second system lies, why it occurred, and what the consequences were.

First the actual break. I could make things easy for myself and refer to the vast literature about "Pauline theology," which a theological lexicon has summed up in one sentence: "His preaching is not just a recapitulation of J.'s words; basically it grapples with an interpretation of the death and resurrection of Christ in conceptual terms that are often hard to understand. . . ."[5] But this does nothing to explain the meaning and effect of the filter, even if it shows how the theme was narrowed down. Yet why was the Pharisee Saul, who later became the apostle Paul, so interested in this part of Rabbi J.'s life?

We often find the key to a man's ideas, theories of life, and convictions in his biography, but here the traditional material fails us exactly as in Rabbi J.'s case. We know nothing about Paul's motives. Just as Rabbi J. first emerges from obscurity in the four gospels when he is baptized and receives his ministry, so Saul the persecutor of Christians first takes shape for us when he experiences his conversion outside Damascus—probably in the throes of an epileptic fit:

"And Saul, yet breathing out threatenings and slaughter against the disciples of the Lord, went unto the high priest, And desired of him letters to Damascus to the synagogues, that if he found any of this way, whether they were men or women, he might bring them bound unto Jerusalem. And as he journeyed, he came near Damascus: and suddenly there shined around him a light from heaven: And he fell to the earth, and heard a voice saying unto him, Saul, Saul, why persecutest thou me? And he said, Who art thou, Lord? And the Lord said, I am J. whom thou persecutest: it is hard for thee to kick against the pricks. And he trembling and astonished said, Lord, what wilt thou have me to do? And the Lord said unto him, Arise, and go into the city, and it shall be told thee what thou must do."[6]

That happened about A.D. 36, a few years after the death of the Rabbi, whose followers, the Nazarenes, Saul, as a Pharisaic scribe, fought with all the means at his disposal. He was an official witness when Stephen, the new sect's first martyr, was stoned to death outside the gates of Jerusalem. Saul was about thirty years old then. Because of his rabid behavior the high priests considered him the right man to stop the sect spreading in Syria and commissioned him to travel to Damascus. Before he arrived there, he experienced his conversion.

We do not know what led to this "Damascus." The Acts of the Apostles represent it as divine intervention and as part of the story of salvation; Christian interpretation likes to think that he was won over by the example of the first Christians; psychologists suspect that unconscious guilt feelings and an inner crisis led to the abrupt change.

The early Christians came to the most reasonable conclusion, although it was quite wrong. They thought that Saul's religious conversion was unreliable and suspected for years that he wanted to infiltrate their ranks as a spy pretending to be a Christian. But Saul, who then called himself Paul—the little one—had undergone a genuine conversion.

The Acts of the Apostles tell us that after his conversion a disciple sought him out and that then the scales fell from Saul's eyes and he was baptized.[7]

The Pharisee "Saul" became a Christian. He joined the Nazarenes.[8] But how did the followers of Rabbi J. reach Damascus, which was hundreds of miles from Jerusalem, only a few years after his death? One naïve suggestion is that some of the early Christians had actually moved there and founded a church, although only the church in Jerusalem is ever mentioned. This cannot be proved or disproved, and in any case we cannot assume that it is the truth. But there is another possibility.

If Saul vigorously persecuted the Essenes connected with the Zealots, who are lumped together in the Acts of the Apostles under the generic name "Christians," then we might suspect that Essenes who were not eyewitnesses of Rabbi J. had lived in Damascus long before J. came on the scene. We know that this was actually so from the Damascus Document, and Saul's baptism confirms it. Just as John the Baptist summoned people to baptism as confirmation of their change of mind, Saul had himself baptized after his experience at Damascus. A ring was closed. If Rabbi J. preached the doctrine of the Essenes, Saul's conversion could logically mean only that he was converted to the teaching of the Essenes.

But then the unforeseeable happened. The movement's biggest enemy suddenly took over the role of propagandist. He now began to propagate the sect with the same intensity with which he had once persecuted it. The original church in Jerusalem treated him with suspicion. There were disputes; Paul had to justify himself; he had his failures, but in the end he alone was the victor.

The Acts of the Apostles only hint cautiously at the disputes and write the history of the early church from Paul's point of view, for history is always written by the victor. In Acts the very things that were not logical consequences were described as if they were. Paul and

Acts make a divine event out of the break, and fulfillment out of repudiation of the past.

For Paul preached two things in the name of Rabbi J., whom he had never seen, that contradict the very basis of his teaching. The man who said of himself, "If any other man thinketh that he hath whereof he might trust in the flesh, I more: Circumsized the eighth day, of the stock of Israel, of the tribe of Benjamin, an Hebrew of the Hebrews; as touching the law, a Pharisee,"[9] justifies his conversion with a sentence in which he not only separates himself from his past, but also from the Essenes' strict adherence to the law and the teaching of Rabbi J.: ". . . not having mine own righteousness, which is of the law, but that which is through the faith of Christ, the righteousness which is of God by faith."[10]

In his search for a merciful God he rejects the law and with it his Pharisaic past, and we might suspect that everything he does and writes only serves to dominate his past, that his whole life as a "servant of Christ" is no more than a life that stands under the shadow of a past unknown to us, that he only used the "case" of Rabbi J. to solve the "case" of Paul.

The second difference is that he is still alive and the teaching of Rabbi J. does not interest him at all. He mentions none, absolutely none of the meager facts supplied in the gospels.[11]

The only thing which Paul considers important is the Jew J.'s ignominious death, which destroyed all hopes of liberation by a Messiah. He makes the victorious Christ out of the failed Jewish Messiah, the living out of the dead, the son of God out of the son of man.

Everything that must have been anathema to an orthodox Jew like Rabbi J. becomes the gospel message in Paul. The suffering Messiah of faith replaces the conquering Messiah of the Jewish people; the transference of a man to heaven, which can only have come from Greek mythological ideas, replaces the "servant of God" on earth, as Isaiah still understood the Messiah; Paul preaches that God-Yahweh is not the one and only God, a concept inconceivable in the Jewish religion. He professes a triune God, a trinity that is yet one. Paul and the evangelist John thus create a syncretism out of monotheism, and Heinz Zahrnt remarks: "Paul especially—John is usually looked on a little more favorably—becomes the 'corrupter of the gospel of Jesus.'"

Twelve

FROM SCAPEGOAT
TO LAMB OF GOD

I‌N his book about the historical J., Heinz Zahrnt writes: "Nowadays J. and Paul are placed so far apart by many theologians that scarcely any historical continuity seems to exist between them. William Wrede writes: 'J. knows nothing about the one and only thing that matters to Paul.' And of Paul he says, vice versa: 'In comparison with J. he is a new phenomenon, as new as it is possible, given a broad common background. He is far more distant from J. than J. himself was from the noblest creations of Jewish piety.' But this simply means that with Paul Christianity had begun for the second time. Wrede says as much, too. He calls Paul 'the second founder of Christianity.' For Paul introduced into Christianity the ideas that were to prove the most powerful and influential in its history. Consequently the discontinuity between the historical J. and the Christ of the church became so great that any unity between the two is scarcely recognizable."[1]

Wrede, too, supported by a large number of independent experts, thinks that Paul only used the reports about Rabbi J. as an excuse for propagating his own ideas. He writes: "This picture of Christ did not spring from the impression J.'s personality made on Paul. Scholars have often claimed that it did, but have never proved it. There is only one explanation left. Paul already believed in such a heavenly being, in a divine

Christ, before he believed in J. . . . And is this belief, for Paul the essence of religion, the framework for the edifice of his piety, without which it would collapse, supposed to be the continuation or modification of J.'s gospel? What is left now of the gospel that Paul is supposed to have understood?"[2]

This question must be asked and answered, if we look at Christianity from its beginning, and not from its end. Lexicon phrases such as "the mixture of the christocentric message of salvation with the demands of the law was a great danger for the early Christian Church."[3] turn the fact upside down, like a magnifying glass held too far away. It was not the christocentric message of salvation that was mixed with the demands of the law, but the other way round. The crisis in the early Christian church came when Paul confronted the loyalty to the law demanded by Rabbi J. with the order to free themselves from belief in the father and so from the law.

What Paul proclaimed as "Christianity" was sheer heresy which could not be based on the Jewish or Essene faith, or on the teaching of Rabbi J. But, as Schonfield says: "The Pauline heresy became the foundation of Christian orthodoxy and the legitimate church was disowned as heretical."[4]

Yet how could a heresy convince even the men who had known Rabbi J. personally and who must have seen that Paul taught something quite different from their Messiah?

Traditional theology naturally denies the possibility of a deliberate reinterpretation of the original and speaks instead of a purely logical development of Rabbi J.'s teaching by Paul.

The argument that Paul would scarcely have succeeded if he had really taught something different from what the early church believed actually has a good deal in its favor. Here it is possible to quote sentences such as this from a biblical lexicon: "Since the discovery of the Qumran scrolls scholars have repeatedly referred to the striking parallels in language and content between the Pauline epistles and the Qumran literature,"[5] or this from the Viennese Judaist Kurt Schubert: "The most obvious similarity between Paul's theology and the Qumran texts is the deep consciousness of sin common to both of them . . . the dualism of light and darkness which plays a large part in the scriptures of St. John is also characteristic of Paul's theology . . ."[6]— sentences, in other words, that start from the mutual dependence of Rabbi J. and Paul on Qumran, and guarantee the continuity of the tradition in the field of incontrovertible philological analysis, proving a connection rather than a break.

But it would not be the first time that someone took over an ideology and a terminology in order to turn it into something different. Rabbi J.'s disciples had reached rock bottom. The hope that one of their group would be the Messiah, the savior of the people and King of Israel, was past. Their master's death remained a mystery to them, and the gospel according to St. Mark, the oldest New Testament after St. Paul's epistles, contains no expression of joy at the resurrection, only despair and horror: "And they went out quickly, and fled from the sepulchre; for they trembled and were amazed: neither said they any thing to any man; for they were afraid."[7]

Certainly they went on hoping, just as the Jews had hoped for the Messiah for centuries and had always been disappointed. They waited for the end of the world that the apocalyptic visions promised, but nothing happened.

Paul arrives in the midst of this situation of disappointed hopes with a message that gives them renewed hope. He explains the very thing that the members of the sect could not explain. He speaks of the master's death. No hope can be linked with the Rabbi's life, for he is dead. That is why it does not interest Paul. He preaches the idea of the suffering Messiah, which is completely alien to Judaism, by making the servant of God mentioned in Isaiah refer to Rabbi J., who "took our sins upon him."

A strange mixture of Jewish and Greek ideas leads to Paul's Christology. "The Lamb of God, that taketh away the sins of the world," reminds us of the literal scapegoat that was sacrificed for the sins of the people on the highest Jewish holy day, the Day of Atonement, and whose blood was scattered on the Atonement Plate so as to symbolize the absolution of people and priests. The high priests then laid their hands on a second scapegoat which thus assumed all the sins of the people, intentional or unintentional. Then the goat, which now bore the sins of the people, was chased into the desert.

This vicarious expiation of sin by sacrifice is transferred by Paul to Rabbi J., the "Lamb of God" that taketh away the sins of the world, although human sacrifice only occurred in Israel in the earliest times. But now he gets into difficulties. If Rabbi J. is the son of God—whatever we understand by that—God has to make atonement with himself, an idea that is also alien to Judaism. The controversial idea that God had to make atonement with "his" blood, with himself, that God in other words had to sacrifice himself, would never occur to a Jew. Yahweh, God the Father, possessed every quality ranging from rage and revenge to atonement, but for the Ineffable to sacrifice himself so as to be reconciled with his creation lies outside the bounds of credibility. God had already made his covenant with the people of Israel.

A quite different kind of God emerges here, a God who has an adversary, a God who reconquers the fallen world of Satan. This is not the God of the Jews, even though in the Book of Job God makes a bet with Satan about Job—an age-old reminiscence of Lucifer, who seduced Eve as the snake. Paul thinks dualistically and so makes contact with one aspect of Essene thinking. The Essenes, too, were familiar with the primeval dual principle, which they paraphrased with light and darkness, and which showed the influence of Persian religions.

The idea of resurrection is also a Gentile one. The Bible is familiar with reincarnation. Thus John the Baptist is looked on as the reincarnation of Elijah[8] and Rabbi J. as the reincarnation of the dead Baptist,[9] but in neither case is it a resurrection from the dead.

The New Testament itself twice points out that the

supposedly physically resurrected Rabbi J. did not have the same appearance as the living one. On Easter Monday Mary Magdalene took him for a gardener, and the disciples at Emmaus[m] walked with him for hours, ate with him, and only recognized him by the Essene gesture of breaking bread. Here too everything remains within the framework of Jewish thinking. A man could be reborn "of water and the spirit,"[n] but this rebirth was a mystery, just as Paul, too, died and was resurrected in Christ, but that did not mean a resurrection from the dead, which was announced for the end of time.

These ideas of resurrection and reincarnation are now carried a stage further by Paul, who links them with the Greek idea of deification. True, Elijah rose up to heaven in a fiery chariot; we read it in the Old Testament. But no Jew around the time of Christ's birth would have dared to think that God took a co-regent in heaven. That would have been sheer heresy, and the only reason we do not recognize it as such is that we have become accustomed as "Christians" not to see the "Trinity" of Father, Son, and Holy Ghost as polytheism, although it must appear so to every Jew.

This syncretic mixture of Jewish tradition and Greek ideas—admitted by all theologians—obviously appeared acceptable to the Jewish Christians in Jerusalem, for otherwise they would have been left without an explanation of Rabbi J.'s death. With Paul's aid, they were able to transfer their lost hope in Rabbi J. to hope in Christ, the spiritual Messiah. Rabbi J.'s life was replaced by the teaching of Christ. The failure of a life was transformed into the success of a divine plan for salvation.

As the proverb says, one may as well be hung for a sheep as a lamb. Once the Jewish Christians had accepted these monstrosities, they could equally well accept Paul's next claim, that redemption was no longer dependent on observing the Mosaic law.

After a tussle Paul managed to convince the representatives of the new sect in Jerusalem that even circumcision which corresponded to baptism in the Christian church, was no longer necessary for salvation.[12] Circumcision, the symbol of Judaism, was abolished by Paul. The decisive step from Jewish sect to universal religion was taken. Albert Schweitzer writes in his book *The Mystique of the Apostle Paul:* "Paul's achievement is that he thought his way through from the evangelical and early Christian belief in salvation through Christ and the coming kingdom to belief in J. as the future Messiah in such a way that he removed its temporal limitation and arrived at a version in which it is valid for all time."[13]

That is undoubtedly true. The Jew J.'s teaching became universal and timeless through Paul and only through Paul. By a brilliant revaluation of all values that are sacred to a Jew, Paul, the former opponent, "redeemed" the teaching of a sect from the arrogant narrowness of a chosen religion and a chosen people who awaited the coming of the Lord in the wilderness. But I should add that he did it not because he was impressed by Rabbi J.'s teaching, but because he sought a way out of his personal experiences with Judaism as a Pharisee and because of his own guilt complex, to which observance of the law did not seem to provide a solution.

Paul did something that Rabbi J. never did and refused to do. He extended God's promise of salvation to the Gentiles; he abolished the law of Moses, and he prevented direct access to God by introducing an intermediary.

Of course anyone can point out that the gospel according to St. John already puts forward this claim: "No man cometh unto the Father, but by me," but the word "already" is wrong. The earliest texts of the New Testament that have come down to us are the epistle of St. Paul, which were written between the years 50 and 60 B.C., although only half of them are recognized as genuine by scholars. All New Testament scholars agree that the gospels were not definitively edited until after 70 B.C. Thus they already presume the victory of Pauline theology; they see Rabbi J.'s life from the point of view of Pauline "fulfillment"; they interpret the man's life according to the meaning of his death. So all the subsequently introduced references to "the Passion" of Rabbi J. and prophecies of the destruction of the temple, which took place in 70 B.C., can be explained as predictions based on hindsight.

After 70 B.C. St. Paul had won the day against the Jewish Christians with his universal gospel because he had more members abroad in Gentile countries than the church in Jerusalem. History was, as always, the story of the majority to which the past had to adapt itself.

And that, in my opinion, is the second filter. The obscured fate of Rabbi J. is reflected and distorted in the life of Paul of Tarsus. The exemplary death of Rabbi J. is so important to him that he is prepared to depart completely from reality and the Jewish faith in order to end his search for redemption in it. He has arrived at faith in "the Savior" and made his faith triumph—but at the cost of separation from Rabbi J.

"We are a universe away from J., "writes the Orientalist Joel Carmichael.

"If Jesus came 'only to fulfil' the Law and the Prophets;

"If he thought that 'not an iota, not a dot' would 'pass from the Law,' that the cardinal commandment was 'Hear, O Israel, the Lord Our God, the Lord is one,' and that 'no one was good but God';

"If he actually considered himself 'sent only to the lost sheep of the House of Israel,' and thought it wrong 'to take the children's bread and throw it to the dogs';...

"If his undertaking was frustrated and he was executed as a rebel against the state;

"What would he have thought of Paul's handiwork!"[14]

Thirteen

THE FLY
IN THE AMBER

Presumably Christianity as we know it would not have existed without Paul. The original basis was so fundamentally altered by him that its meaning was completely reversed. What interests him about the itinerant preacher's life is his death, not his teaching. He does not ask what led to J.'s death; he only sees what it means to him personally. He turns a man who summoned people to reconciliation with God into the savior. He turns an orthodox Jewish movement into a universal religion which ultimately clashed with Judaism.

In the course of this transference from the Jewish to the Graeco-Roman cultural sphere, a further alienation took place, in addition to Paul's work. True, Palestine had long been influenced and stamped by Hellenism. The theology of the Jew Paul shows that. There were Greek cities and Greek as well as Aramaic was spoken in Palestine. Paul wrote his epistles in Greek, and the New Testament has come down to us only in a Greek version.

But there is a difference between a Jew reading the gospels and the epistles of St. Paul and a Greek reading them. To a Jew the Greek words retain their Jewish meaning. If he reads the Greek word *Christos*, he knows that it is the translation of the word Messiah and also that the literal meaning "anointed one" refers to kings who were anointed. So the word Messiah to a Jew is a synonym for the word king.[1] It is not to a Greek, because in his range of experience kings were not anointed.

To him the word *Christos* is the shell of a word without associations, a cipher that has to be endowed with content.

It also makes a difference whether a Jew or a non-Jew reads the concept "son of God." Admittedly both understand at once what is said. It is a clear description of a relationship; one immediately associates something with it. But that is just where the misunderstanding comes in, for each of them understands something different by "the son of God." In their civilization the Greeks, who were used to the idea of the gods of Olympus mating with the children of earth and begetting children, had no difficulty in incorporating the concept into their world. Even a Roman, whose rulers were worshiped as divinities, could make something of the idea. And because they could incorporate the idea into their worlds they did not ask about its original meaning in the original language.

So the concept of "the son of God" led to a misunderstanding which had undreamed-of consequences. Anyone with only a superficial knowledge of the East knows that the Orientals like picturesque speech. For them the photographer is the 'father of the picture.' The impersonal relationship between producer and product is reproduced in a flowery image; abstract relations are represented by paraphrases. A simple liar is a son of lies, and anyone who can go one better becomes a father of lies. The phrase "son of God" is on the very same level of speech and thought.

In Semitic linguistic usage this description says nothing more than that a bond exists between a man and God. A Jew would never even dream of thinking that the son of God meant a genuine relationship between a father and a son. A son of God is a blessed man, a chosen vessel, a man who does what God wants. Any attempt to take this image literally and so deduce the divinity of the son contradicts the facts.

The Old Testament gives many examples of how the concept of the son of God was understood. For example, it was the normal coronation formula for kings, intended to show that the Messiah, the anointed king, was "begotten" in the name of God., i.e., that he was appointed by Yahweh. As it says in the psalm:

> Yet have I set my king upon my holy hill of Zion.
> I will declare the decree the Lord hath said unto me.
> Thou art my son; this day I have begotten thee.[2]

When David was promised that his descendants would become kings, too, it was paraphrased in the Bible as follows: "And when thy days shall be fulfilled, and thou shalt sleep with thy fathers, I will set up thy seed after thee, which shall proceed out of thy bowels, and I will establish his kingdom. . . .

And in another psalm it says of David:

> I have found David my servant; with my holy oil have I
> anointed him. . . . He shall cry unto me, Thou art my father,
>   my God, and the rock of my salvation.
> Also I will make him my first-born, higher than the kings
>   of the earth.[4]

According to the Jewish way of thinking, "the son of God" can also apply to a whole people. Thus Moses is told to say to Pharaoh: "Thus saith the Lord, Israel is my son, even my firstborn. And I say unto thee, let my son go that he may serve me. . . ."[5] Or again in Jeremiah: "For thus saith the Lord . . . I am a father to Israel, and Ephraim is my firstborn."[6]

Joel Carmichael sums it up as follows: "Most Christians take this concept of Jesus as the Son of God for granted as having been implicit in Jesus' view of himself. But a moment's glance at the Gospels will show how it provided a matrix for the whole process of magnification. . . . The title 'son of God' was of course entirely familiar to Jews in Jesus' life-time and indeed for centuries before; all Jews were sons of God; this was in fact what distinguished them from other people. . . . More specifically the phrase was applied to eminent personages generally, and especially to kings, celestial emissaries, and so forth. . . . During the postexilic period in Jewish history the word was further applied to any particularly pious man; ultimately it became common in reference to the Righteous Man and the Prince.

"In all these cases of Jewish usage, the phrase was plainly a metaphor to emphasize a particularly close connection between individual virtue and divine authority. The concept of any man's actually having been biographically engendered by the disembodied majesty of Yahweh, God of the Universe, would not only have been a grotesque extravagance in a Jewish milieu; it would actually have been unintelligible."[7]

But at the moment when early Christianity moved on to other linguistic patterns and modes of thought, and began to free itself from its Jewish origins, the impossible became possible. Rabbi J. could only be turned into the son of God outside Judaism, because people took the metaphor literally as "the inspired word of God" and no longer knew or wanted to know its real meaning. For even to mention the "only begotten," i.e., the only son of God, contradicts the various firstborn sons in the Old Testament. (However, the only place in the whole Bible where the actual phrase "only begotten son" occurs is in St. John, whose gospel is considered to be the one most strongly influenced by Hellenism.)

The church did not take the easy way out; it only made the divine nature of Christ dogma and included the doctrine of the Trinity in the Creed after lengthy disputes. This decision was the result of theological thinking and speculation, but not a reflection of what stood in the New Testament.

Theology began to make itself independent. Admittedly its thesis is that it was oriented solely toward the Bible and nothing else. But actually even the first centuries of the church's existence saw the beginning of a process which has continued to this day—the process of the ideologization of the faith, which, working on the slogan that inconvenient truths ought not to exist, goes back to the sources and makes whatever it wants out of them. Schonfield's harsh words, "The formula of the Trinity, 'God, the Father, God the Son, and God the Holy Ghost,' is an unjustifiable distortion by Pauline religious dogma,'"[8] were put rather more elegantly by Goethe in his *Westöstlichen Divan:*

> J.... thought secretly
> about the one and only God;
> whoever made him [J.] a God
> offended against God's holy will.

The transformation of the Jew J. into a God is not the only alienation that took place during the passage from one cultural sphere to another. The miracles, too, are additions from a foreign culture that sees proof of the extraordinary in the extraordinary deeds performed by its heroes. It is quite common in religious history to read about founders of religions who were supposed to have been born of a virgin, whose death was accompanied by an earthquake at least, and who were taken up into heaven after death. But none of that is Jewish. And what is even more important, none of that has any connection with Rabbi J., after whose title his followers called themselves Christians.

It would be easy to quote still more examples showing that the change from Jewish sect to universal religion distorted and falsified many ideas, beginning with the symbolical "overloading" of the phrase "son of man," which comes from the apocalyptic vision in the Book of Daniel and is connected with Qumran, down to the misunderstanding of a normal Passover meal, which, divorced from its ordinary context, became the sacrament of the Last Supper. The idea of the son of God is only one example of how the second filter worked.

In my opinion, it can do no harm if we take one more general look at the way in which the two filters worked, for everything is different after Qumran. Even if the theologians were able to say in the past that the influences of Hellenism and the Christian tradition could be established as alterations of what was originally meant, but no one knew what was originally meant, this simply is not true today.

It makes no difference how closely we connect Rabbi J. with the Essene community at Qumran. The fact that he was influenced by it in his actions and even in individual words he used can no longer be denied, unless we deny all the principles of scholarly comparisons, analysis, and methods.

Rabbi J. had certainly carefully considered all the different religious ideas of his day; like Paul, he was a man who sought the truth where it was to be found; and the truth men seek is not to be found in a single place, not even when the place is called Qumran. But he did find the cardinal point of his truth and his teaching among the Essenes; comparison of the Dead Sea scrolls and the New Testament proves it. That is his point of departure, his spiritual and intellectual home.

I have tried to show that there were reasons for concealing his connection with Qumran. The circle of his disciples was responsible for this. They were actual eyewitnesses and fellow combatants, who were in awe of the mystery and afraid of persecution, and so did their best to explain the continuity of a sect in the person of Rabbi J. by his uniqueness.

They obscured J.'s life until only disconnected reflections of his life and teaching remained. Since the Dead Sea finds, we can throw light on these dark passages again.

His death remained unexplained and inexplicable to the disciples. In this situation Paul arrived and gave the despairing group their hope back. The important thing was not the life of Rabbi J., which was obscured anyhow, but his death. It was no longer the end of *a* life, but the beginning of *the* life.

As if with a magnifying glass Paul enlarged a stage of life that confronts every man—death—and interpreted it as an act of atonement by God that benefited everybody. He saw the life of a man as if through a polarization filter and eliminated all the reflections and rays that might prejudice this exaltation of a stage in life. He set aside everything about Rabbi J. that made him a Jew. His Christ no longer has any earthly Jewish characteristics, he has become the savior of all mankind.

Halfway between Judaism and Hellenistic influences, Paul drew a picture of Rabbi J. that could be an abstract painting. Everyone who saw it rediscovered his own thoughts and impressions in it; everyone interpreted it according to his own experience of life; everyone was free to give the picture a name. Even if it was hung upside down, it was still a picture that made an impression on people. The Pauline problem picture became a universal religion, and for two thousand years people have been trying to interpret and understand it, to overpaint and restore it.

The historical Rabbi J. is hardly mentioned any more. The clique of theologians and churches who are considered the trustees of his heritage is not interested in his faith, but in faith in him. But what they look on as the living heritage is not the original one. What they expound as true Christianity is something quite different. "The triumph of Paul meant the definitive obliteration of the historical Jesus. The historical Jesus has reached us embedded in Christianity like a fly in amber."[9] (Carmichael.)

Fourteen

RABBI J.'S ANSWERS

W E must bear in mind that every institution, as I said at the beginning, has an innate tendency to settle down and become complacent, and tries to give itself a value per se. Institutions tend to become monopolies.

Just as the trade unions once fought for the workers' right to strike, yet later took the right away from the workers and gave the institution of the trade union a monopoly on striking, the institution of the church has not escaped this monopolization. What was once God's mercy, available to anyone who desired it, became a means of grace offered by the church, available only to those who belonged to it and lived according to its rules. And as institutions develop their own laws which ensure their ability to function even when their original function has disappeared, they all need periodic revisions, the purpose of which is to check whether the "functionaries" are really doing what they ought, and not what they want, to do.

In its outward form the church, too, is nothing more than an institution—indeed it is one of the oldest. It has needed revisions and reinterpretations just like other organizations. It is not sacrosanct or untouchable. And so down the ages it has had to accept reinterpretations or reject them whether it was willing to or not. All these reinterpretations were based on the assumption that the church was no longer fulfilling the mission with which it had been entrusted in the New Testament.

People continually measured the present against Rabbi J.'s original mission and often only the accident of a historical constellation or the power game—frequently political—has decided whether the church recognized its critics as reformers or condemned them as heretics. For what was really Rabbi J.'s original mission was not established so long as people considered the New Testament as a whole and did not know which texts or passages came closest in content to his teaching.

Since the discovery of the Dead Sea scrolls, we possess, for the first time in nearly two thousand years, documents for comparison which lie outside the ecclesiastical system and outside the Bible itself, and are historically older than the twenty-seven canonical scriptures of the New Testament. We are not fobbed off with suppositions about Rabbi J.'s spiritual and intellectual background. We can compare his supposed background with the facts.

To repeat a quotation: "If historical research has succeeded in proving that an irreconcilable antithesis existed between the historical J. and Christ as preached and thus that faith in J. had no basis in J. himself . . . it would mean the end of all Christology. But I am convinced that even then we theologians would find a way out—but either we would be lying then or we are lying now."[1]

I had an answer ready to this quotation from Heinz Zahrnt when I first used it at the end of the account of the effect and operation of the first filter (cf. Chapter 10), but first I wanted to write about the second filter that had altered the picture again and even more fundamentally. I know that it would be possible to write massive tomes about the second filter alone and still more examples, but an answer can be given now, for the man who is not prepared to draw the logical conclusions from the foregoing would not do so even if he were given more facts.[2]

I am convinced that the answer is that an irreconcilable antithesis between the historical J. and Christ as preached actually does exist. The Christ whom the church preaches has nothing in common with the historical Rabbi J., not even his name.

If Church and theologians are really concerned with the historical Rabbi J., then they ought to leave out the heathen miracle stories and speak soberly and realistically about a man whose search for God led him to a strictly orthodox and ascetic desert sect, who, in expectation of God's intervention, altered his way of thinking and had himself baptized; who then traveled through the country, proclaiming the call to repentance to his fellow countrymen—and no one else; whose disciples looked on him as the God-designated liberator from the Romans and coming King of Israel, the Messiah, and were themselves persecuted as Zealots. They ought to relate that this mission of political liberation, which could only come about if the people obeyed God's Law, failed with the arrest and execution of Rabbi J. by the Romans, and that his disciples fled in despair.

If church and theologians are really concerned with the historical Rabbi J., then they ought to speak of a man who called for the complete abandonment of possessions so that the law of Moses could be kept more strictly; they should depict him as a man who was an out-and-out Jew and understood the coming of the kingdom of God not as a spiritual event, but as the independence of the chosen Jewish people brought about by piety; who addressed Yahweh as father because according to the actual Bible stories God had described himself as the father of Israel, but who as a Jew would never have dreamt of looking on himself as the physical son of God or appearing as mediator between man and God.

If church and theologians were really concerned with the historical Jew J., then they should have spoken of an exceptional man who fascinated other men and undoubtedly possessed unusual faculties and—like the Essenes—understood something of the art of healing. They should have told the world about a man who spoke differently and more convincingly about Yahweh, the invisible and only God and his relation to man.

If church and theologians were really concerned with the historical J., they should have said more about God and less about Rabbi J. For they ought to think and perceive things in the Jewish way before they speak as Christians.

Instead they "preach" an obscured and distorted "Christ" originated by history and tradition, in whom Rabbi J. would recognize himself with astonishment and horror, if at all. They speak of the Savior and the resurrected J., they call him the Son of God, who takes our sins upon him, the mediator, redeemer, and Lord; today in the Creed they still profess that he was born of a virgin and went up to heaven, where he sits at the right hand of God—in not a single word of which would Rabbi J. recognize himself and say: Yes, that is I.

They talk of the Last Supper and the New Testament, of love and redemption, of Our Father and the Sermon on the Mount—and each time Rabbi J. would stand up and say: Yes, but it wasn't like that at all.

They talk of God in Christ, of his uniqueness and the exemplary sin-free life he led—and each time Rabbi J. would take a step backward and say: I was a devout Jew like other Jews. I sought God and I do not know whether I found him—my God, my God, why hast thou forsaken me?

When church and theologians speak about him, they either do so like Luther four hundred and fifty years ago and say: "I believe that J. Christ, the true God born of the Father in eternity and also true man born of the Virgin Mary, is my Lord, who hath redeemed me a lost and condemned man,"[3] or they talk with "admittedly, . . . buts" about the dangerous comparison with reality and use the community of the faithful as historical proof: "When the New Testament speaks of J. Christ, it means the J. of faith, admittedly J. himself, but in the form in which the New Testament makes him known to us: J. as Lord and 'object' of the Christian faith."[4] Or the same thing, this time as phrased by a progressive Catholic: "If we want to express anything religiously and theologically meaningful about J. Christ himself today, we cannot do it without also describing the nature of the faith itself as action, which sees J. as the Christ."[5]

But they do not have the courage to admit that their Christ is possibly someone quite different from Rabbi J. and that the historical Rabbi J. differs fundamentally from the one in whom people believe.

Sometimes they even turn the sequence of events around and argue from the end instead of the beginning which establishes the criterion. Thus, according to Bonhoeffer, the attempt "to separate a synoptic J. from a Pauline Christ is historically and dogmatically doomed to failure. From the dogmatic point of view, if this separation of J. from Christ were possible, the church's message would become an illusion."[6] What if it did? Where does it say that the church's message is right and must be preserved? Does the search for historical truth come to a halt when the existence of an institution is endangered?

Here Bonhoeffer, who otherwise has said a good deal that is worthy of reflection about a "Christianity without religion," is completely caught in the ideological screen according to which inconvenient truths ought not to exist. If the historical J. were not also the J. who is preached, he writes, "the substance would be taken away from the Church."[7]

Consequently he claims that "the present Christ . . . is the historical Christ."[8] That is simply a statement of faith, with which to calm angry Christians and bolster up the institution. It has nothing to do with reality.

Nevertheless, I am convinced that church and

theologians look upon themselves as the legitimate heirs and trustees of Rabbi J.'s heritage and will not recognize a single argument that might call into question their existence or their convictions, for here the wonderful function of perpetual excuses (mentioned by Zahrnt) begins to operate and constantly produces arguments based on the wrong plane. Presumably the church and its theologians will still rely on their *idée fixe* about the Enlightenment and say that all reproaches and arguments were met in the last century. Using this defense they once again shelve a decision, which has long since confronted the vast majority of Christians, who consider the church and Christianity to be untrustworthy and dishonest.

I have a certain sympathy with the church's attitude, for what institution likes to see the justification for its existence argued away, if it can prevent it with the counterargument that its existence and faith have lasted for two thousand years. But in that case the theologians are not only lying now, but they would be lying then. For they are not in the least concerned with historical "truth," but only with their prestige and their existence. They use Rabbi J. as an excuse for an entirely different faith.

No one should assume that churches ever dissolve themselves because of error, even given good reason. That would be an illusion, however justified the dissolution might be. But I say that they should be honest and either admit that they have to think things out again or that they are freeing themselves by a new "creed" from the misleading conception that they still represent the true and original goals and intentions of the man after whom they call themselves. That would be an honorable decision, and consequently what the churches would still describe as religion even then would have to be honest.

Then religion would be nothing but man's subsequent reflections about J.'s origin, life, death, and meaning, without such personal reflection being arbitrarily withdrawn from the discussion as "revelation" or rejected as error.

Even then the churches would still call themselves "Christian" for they can no more escape from two thousand years of history than the individual can. But then the founder of their religion would be Paul of Tarsus and not Rabbi J., who has even had his Jewish name Joshua taken away from him.[9]

NOTES

CHAPTER ONE

1. Letter from Lentulus, who was, according to ancient sources, an official senior to Pilate.
2. Ibid.
3. Ibid.
4. John 2:1–2.
5. *Das Neue Testament für Menschen unserer Zeit:* translated by H. Riethmüller, Quell Verlag, 1964.
6. *NT 68,* Wurttemberg Bible Institute, 1967.
7. Shalom Ben Chorin, *Jesus—Bruder Jesus—Der Nazarener in jüdischer Sicht,* List Verlag, 1967, pp. 84–85.
8. Matthew 13:10–13, 16.
9. Matthew 13:18, 19.
10. Matthew 7:28–29.

CHAPTER TWO

1. Josephus, *Antiquities of the Jews,* XX, 9, 1, para. 200.
2. Tacitus, *Annals,* XV, 44 (written between 115 and 117 B.C. Another profane source that tells us about a "Messianic movement" in Rome is Suetonius, who never mentions Christians or Jesus by name, although he is referring to Christians.)
3. Matthew 10:34
4. Macmillan, 1962.
5. Luke 22:35–36.

6. Carmichael, *The Death of Jesus*, Macmillan, New York, 1962, p. 152.
7. Ibid., p. 157.
8. Ibid., p. 89–90.
9. Ibid., p. 90.

CHAPTER THREE

1. Flavius Josephus, *The Jewish War*, quoted here in G.A. Williamson's translation, Penguin Classics, 1970, Ch. 7, pp. 125–30. Flavius Josephus was born in Jerusalem in 37 B.C. He was a Jewish commander in Galilee during the Jewish rebellion against the Romans, 66–8 B.C., went over to the Romans, and died in Rome in 100 B.C.
2. From Edmund Wilson, *The Scrolls from the Dead Sea*, New York, Oxford University Press, 1955.
3. Luke 9:3–6.
4. John 12:6.
5. John 3:25. The difference between the single "baptism" in the Jordan and the repeated ritual washing at Qumran postulated by many theologians is not convincing. Both were symbolic of purification and signified rejection of evil, as it says in the Manual of Discipline: "No one is to go into water in order to obtain the purity of holy men. For men cannot be purified except they repent of their evil" (Manual of Discipline, 5:13, 14). The only difference is that the men of Qumran performed this "purification" daily, whereas according to the NT baptism as a sign of conversion took place only once. One does not exclude the other.
6. Matthew 5:37.
7. Philo, *Quod omnis probus liber sit*, Ch. 12. Philo of Alexandria, Jewish Hellenistic philosopher, was born in Alexandria some thirty to twenty years B.C.

8. For further details see Albert Schweitzer, *Geschichte de Leben-Jesu-Forschung*, Siebenstern-Taschenbuch, 1966, Vol. I, pp. 79 ff.

9. Ibid., p. 191.

10. Ibid., p. 195.

11. Pliny, *Naturalis Historia* V, XVII, 73. Pliny the Elder, born c. A.D. 23, died during the eruption of Vesuvius that destroyed Pompeii.

CHAPTER FIVE

1. 1 Maccabees 1:12.

2. 1 Maccabees 1:56; 2:27–31.

3. Kurt Schubert, *Die Gemeinde vom Toten Meer, Munich*, 1956, pp. 20 ff.

4. War Scroll 1:1–5 (quoted from Theodor H. Gaster, *The Dead Sea Scriptures*, Doubleday, New York, 1956, p. 281).

5. Manual of Discipline 1:9–11 (see Note 4).

6. Ibid., 3:19.

7. Ibid., 3:15.

8. John 1:1–5.

9. Mark 1:5.

10. John 1:28.

11. John 1:35–39.

12. Mark 1:12, 13.

CHAPTER SIX

1. Malachi 3:23.

2. Matthew 3:1–3.

3. A cantilena is a kind of melody akin to plainsong. The Masoretic text means the critical glosses on the Hebrew text of the Old Testament made by the Masoretes, Jewish scribes of the seventh to tenth centuries.

4. Shalom Ben Chorin, *Jesus, bruder Jesus—der Nazarener in jüdischer sicht*, List Verlag, 1967, p. 45.

5. Luke 3:4.

6. Manual of Discipline 8:13, 14.

7. Millar Burrows, *Die Schriftrollen vom Toten Meer*, Verlag C. H. Beck, Munich, 1958, Vol. I, p. 271.

8. Burrows, Vol. I, p. 272 (see Note 7).

9. Kurt Schubert, *Die Schriftrollen vom Toten Meer*, p. 110.

10. Luke 1:80.

11. Josephus, *Jewish War*, II.

CHAPTER SEVEN

1. John M. Allegro, *The Dead Sea Scrolls*, Penguin, 1956.

2. A part of the Essene library had, in fact, been found even earlier. At the beginning of the third century, Origenes wrote that he had found a translation of the Psalms and other Greek and Hebrew books in an earthenware vessel near Jericho. Nearly six hundred years later the Patriarch of Seleukia said that he knew books of the Old Testament and other scriptures 'that were discovered in a cave near Jericho' (*The Shrine of the Book and its Scrolls*, published by the Israel Museum, Jerusalem, 1966, p. 1).

3. Manual of Discipline 1:14 ff.

4. Book of Jubilees 6:36–38, and the Book of Enoch. The figure 364 is the product of multiplying the days of the week by the weeks in a year (7 times 52). Although this does not tally exactly with the solar year of 365.25 days, it nevertheless ensures the regular return of the days of the week, including the Sabbath, and can easily be corrected by a leap year. The lunar year, on the other hand, consisting of twelve revolutions of the moon, has 354 days and is eleven days shorter than the solar year. But since the Passover

feast, dependent on the Spring moon, is always celebrated on the 15th day of the month of Nisan, it is only possible to keep the date constant by a complicated system of additional days and even additional months. As a result feast days are constantly moved about. Thus according to the lunar calendar the 15th of Nisan, for example, does not always fall on the same day of the week. According to the solar calendar, as used by the Essenes, the Sabbath and the Passover Feast always fell on Tuesday-Wednesday.

5. War Scroll II, 1 ff.

6. Kurt Schubert, *Die Gemeinde vom Toten Meer*, Munich, 1956, p. 53.

7. According to the Qumran Manual of Discipline, it was even forbidden to relieve oneself on the Sabbath. The Damascus scroll on the other hand, which also forms part of the Essene library, modifies the strictness of the Qumran rules on various points, for example the prohibition of swearing, divorce and the rules for the Sabbath. In Ch. 10, 15 ff., unlike Qumran, only the normally current Sabbath rules are stressed. Thus in the compilation of the Essene scriptures we must assume different stages of development and starting points, as well as the possibility of a different interpretation by members of the sect.

8. Matthew 12:1–8, Mark 2:23–28, and Luke 6:1.

9. Millar Burrows, p. 71.

10. Shalom Ben Chorin, *J., Bruder J.*, pp. 160–61. Re the calendar question of also Thierry Maertens, *Heidnisch-jüdische Wurzeln der Christlichen Feste*, Grünewald Verlag, Mainz, 1965, pp. 86–95.

Maertens writes as follows about the date of the Last Supper: "In the year of Jesus's Last Supper the Passover feast of the 15th Nisan according to the permanent (i.e., solar) calendar fell on a Tuesday as prescribed; but according to the lunar calendar used by the Temple the Passover feast fell on the following Friday. Christ celebrated the Passover meal with his apostles on Tuesday evening . . ." (p. 91). The reason why some authors give the date of the Passover feast as the 14th Nisan and others as the 15th Nisan and similarly make either Tuesday or Wednesday the first day of the week in the solar calendar may be because according to our calendar system days in the east are reckoned from evening to evening and so have two dates.

Details of the various calendar systems and conversion formulas can be found in *Der Kalender* by Walter F. Wislicenus, Verlag Teubner, Leipzig, 1905.

11. Mark 14:13–15.

12. Ben Chorin (Note 10, p. 161).

13. Manual of Discipline 6:3–13.

14. Manual of Discipline 6:8, 9.

15. Luke 20:24.

16. John 13:14–16.

17. For further details see Ben Chorin (Note 10, pp. 162–66).

CHAPTER EIGHT

1. Matthew 5:13

2. Mark 9:49.

3. Matthew 5:3, in Luther's translation.

4. *The New Testament*, translated by Franz Sigge, Fischer Bücherei, 1958.

5. *The New English Bible*, Oxford/Cambridge University Press, 1961.

6. *NT 68, Württembergische Bibelanstalt*, Stuttgart, 1967.

7. Quell Verlag, Stuttgart, 1964, translator Helmut Riethmüller.

8. *Das Neue Testament*, by Jörg Zink, Krauz Verlag, 1965.

9. Shalom Ben Chorin, J., *Bruder J., der Nazarener in jüdischer Sicht*, List Verlag, 1967, pp. 70–71.

10. Kurt Schubert, *The Dead Sea Community: Its Origins and Its Teachings*, Humanities, 1958.

11. Millar Burrows: *More Light on the Dead Sea Scrolls*, Viking, New York, 1958, p. 95.

12. Matthew 6:9–13.

13. Matthew 24:15, 16.

14. Daniel 11:31.

15. 1 Maccabees 1 ff.

16. Frank Moore Cross, *The Ancient Library of Qumran and Modern Biblical Studies*, New York, 1961, p. 159.

17. Ibid., p. 200.

18. Ibid., p. 204.

19. Luke 2:14.

20. The usual objectives to a comparison of these related passages are as follows:

    1. That owing to the strict Qumran rules neither John the Baptist (Ch. 6) nor J. (if we assume that both of them were Essenes) could have addressed himself to outsiders because that would have meant defilement, and besides, it was a duty to hate the Sons of Darkness:

    2. That the crucial "Christian" message of loving one's enemies in the eighth chapter of the gospel according to St. Matthew is not recorded in the Qumran texts.

    Re Point 1, note the following quotations from the Manual of Discipline which are not restricted to a monastic community:

    "To act truthfully and righteously and justly on earth," (1:5).

    "To bring into a bond of mutual love all who have declared their willingness to carry out the statutes of God" (1:7).

161

"This is the way those spirits operate in the world. The enlightenment of man's heart, the making straight before him all the ways of righteousness and truth . . ." (4:2).

"These are the things that come to man in this world through communion with the spirit of truth." (4:6).

"No one is to engage in discussion or disputation with men of ill repute. . . . With those, however, that have chosen the right path everyone is indeed to discuss matters pertaining to the apprehension of God's truth and of His righteous judgments. . . ." These passages make it clear that the actual rules of the Qumran order provided for a certain missionary and propaganda activity, on roughly the same lines as that carried out by John the Baptist and Jesus. And words in the Manual of Discipline such as ". . . to show how faithfulness may be maintained on earth . . . how, by active performance of justice . . . iniquity may be cleared, and how one can walk with all men with the quality of truth and in conduct appropriate to every occasion . . ." (7:3, 4), sound just like the mission that John and Jesus sought to fulfill.

The summons to join the Essenes is issued to everybody:

"If any man in Israel wish to be affiliated to the formal congregation of the community . . ." (6:13), he is to be examined. The Qumran Manual of Discipline even provides for members of the order meeting outside the community. Such cases were regulated according to recognized Jewish law: "Wherever there be ten men who have been formally enrolled in the community, one who is a priest is not to depart from them." (6:3, also Damascus Document 13:2.)

Lastly the Manual of Discipline also provides for its members practicing a profession. If a man had a year's novitiate behind him and was admitted by a majority, he had to "bring with him all his property and the tools of his profession. These are to be committed to the custody of the community's 'minister of works.' " (6:19.) In other words, the Essenes of Qumran could obviously practice a profession outside the monastery, just as some of Jesus' disciples were and remained fishermen.

Re Point 2: The passage in Matthew 5:43–44 ("You have heard that it hath been said, Thou shalt love thy neighbour and hate thine enemy. But I say unto you, Love your enemies") is usually considered a counterargument by theologians because the Manual of Discipline expressly prescribes its members to hate the "Sons of Darkness." The Sons of Darkness were understood to mean nearly all non-Qumran members. But such a generalization is not admissible according to the Manual of Discipline. The passages quoted under Point 1 show a marked differentiation between the "froward men" (who were to be found in the Temple at Jerusalem) and the others.

But even if hate is demanded in one (the only!) passage in the Manual of Discipline, this should not be made too much of. Even in the New Testament there are some hair-raising passages to set against the commandment to love ones enemies. Jesus curses whole cities, he says he comes to bring a sword and there is not a single example in the New Testament of Jesus himself practicing loving his enemies, apart from the one (the only!) remark in Matthew. The Qumran scrolls are not as uniform as we should like; they are not more uniform than the New Testament itself. Like the Testament scriptures they were not written by one hand at one time, but originated at different stages of development. Consequently there are contradictory sayings in the scrolls, which are still further intensified by the

Damascus Document. This meant that there was considerable latitude in the texts for the Essenes to choose from. Jesus knew this, too, and had to make up his mind about them. For his command to love one's enemies Jesus could appeal to the Manual of Discipline: "I will requite no one with evil, I will pursue men with good, for in God is the judgment over everything that lives. . . ." (10:17, 18; cf. x, 10:23, 11:1–3.)

That agrees with the "passionateness of human love" that Philo of Alexandria attributed to the Essenes and which would also invalidate another counterargument that is usually produced in this connection, namely that Jesus could not possibly have consorted with publicans (agents of the Roman occupying power), beggars, and whores if he had been an Essene. Apart from the question whether these were not precisely the people who might "wish to be affiliated to the formal congregation of the community" (i.e., the Essenes)—the publican Zacchaeus, who climbed a tree in Jericho in order to see Jesus, even gave half his goods away to the poor—apart from that, the Damascus Document contains the specific injunction "to love each man his neighbour like himself; to grasp the hand of the poor, the needy and the stranger; to seek each man the welfare of his fellow." (Damascus Document 6:21.)

As not all the scrolls have come down to us—some were destroyed and others are only fragments—we should be careful about the exclusions we make. If something cannot be pointed to in the scrolls, it is not necessarily against or outside Essene doctrine if it is in the New Testament. Negative proof cannot be furnished from both sides. Still, we prove the relationship between twins by their visible (manifest) similarity and not by their potential (latent) but not demonstrable differences.

CHAPTER NINE

1. Matthew 13:16.
2. Matthew 22:21.
3. Carmichael, p. 125.
4. 1 Maccabees 2:27–31.
5. Yigael Yadin, *Masada,* Hoffmann und Campe, 1967, p. 173.
6. Ibid., p. 174.
7. Ibid., p. 174.
8. Ibid., p. 174.
9. Luke 6:12–16, Matthew 10:1–4, Mark 3:13–19.
10. Friedrich Samuel Rothenberg (ed.), *Männer und Frauen des Neuen Testaments,* Verlag Brockhaus, 1966, p. 55.
11. Matthew 16:17.
12. Carmichael, p. 129-30.

CHAPTER TEN

1. Matthew 27:37.

The initials INRI (Jesus Nazarenus Rex Judaeorum) come from John 19:19 and indicate a later development because of the insertion of Nazarenus. Albert Schweitzer has this to say in his *Leben-Jesu-Forschung:* "The origin of the title can be traced. In the post-Pauline period the Christians were split into factions that were for or against the ascetic way of life. The supporters of asceticism were called after the old Jewish Nazarites (Amos 2:11–12). The reference to the Messianic passage, Isaiah 11:1, which mentions a branch (*nezer*), may also have had an influence on the choice of this title. Nazareans and Nazarenes are etymologically identical with Nazarites. In any case neither of the first two expressions had anything to do with the town of Nazareth originally; if they had, the word would have been Nazarethenes or something similar. As the ascetic group naturally claimed that Jesus was a Nazarite, he was given that epithet. This stage is recorded in the Acts of the Apostles (German version). It describes Christians as Nazareans (Acts 24:5) and also describes Jesus as "a Nazarean" (Acts 2:22; 3:6; 4:10; 6:14; 22:8; 26:9.).

Later the anti-ascetic groups tried hard to paralyze the Nazarite movement inside Christianity. For this purpose they created a "new quasi-historical basis" for the expression and made Jesus come from the town of Nazareth. The proof of this is in the Gospel according to St. Mark which consistently talks of "Nazarenes" . . . and avoids the word "Nazarean." (Siebenstern-Taschenbuch, Vol. II, p. 470.)

2. Thus Heinz Zahrndt: "The historical power that we meet first in the tradition is always the Church. At first we see the picture of the historical figure solely in its mirror. And this picture is decided by the belief that Jesus is the Christ and it is drawn to represent this belief and show it as true. In the process the Church created the story of Jesus as we know it for the first time. It has put words into his mouth that he never spoke and related deeds that he never did." (*Es begann mit Jesus von Nazareth*, Kreuz Verlag, 2d ed., 1960, p. 84.)

The *Praktische Bibellexikon* (Herder Verlag, 1969, col. 389) says, "the Christian church had a creative influence on the formation and extension of the original Jesus tradition owing to its post-crucifixion outlook."

Thus Herbert Braun: "The sources tell us about Jesus in such a way that they assert his importance a priori, that they instruct us in the Christian sense and try to act the missionary . . . the individual evangelists also have clearly outlined theological aims and objects in view which they impress on the oral or written material handed down to them. This means that they make J. talk in a way that conforms to their theological conviction." (*J.—der Mannaus*

Nazareth und seine Zeit, Kreuz Verlag, 1969, pp. 30, 32.)

3. Luke 1:1–3.

4. Matthew 10:34.

5. Luke 22:36.

6. Kreuz Verlag, Stuttgart, 2d ed., 1960, p. 112.

CHAPTER ELEVEN

1. Hermann Raschke has recently tried to prove the unhistorical-
ness of J. (in *Jesusbilder in theologischer Sicht*, edited by
Karlheinz Deschner, List Verlag, 1966). The result is not
so original as the method. Raschke starts with the ambig-
uity of Hebrew words, which are written without vowels
and which, given different vowels, have another meaning.
Now Raschke thinks that the writers of the NT deliberately used this method to describe a secret doctrine intelligible only to initiates, which he links with Qumran.
Accordingly proper names and whole events were only bear-
ers of a special meaning which vocalized conventionally
sounds quite harmless (and corresponds to the text of the
NT as translated today). Although Raschke may have gone
much too far in his conclusions, he once again draws our
attention, in way that deserves our thanks, to the too often
disregarded process of the symbolization of individual letters and combinations of letters that lies absolutely in
Jewish thinking and that we find again for example in
Revelation.

2. *Praktisches Bibellexikon*, a collaboration between Catholic and
Evangelical theologians, edited by A. Grabner-Haider,
Herder Verlag, Freiberg, 1969, under Qumran, Col. 908.

3. Edmund Wilson, *The Scrolls from the Dead Sea*, New York,
Oxford University Press, 1955, quoted by Millar Burrows,
Mehr Klarheit über die Schriftrollen, C. H. Beck, Munich,
1958, p. 33.

4. *Die Bibel und ihre Welt, eine Enzyklopädie zur heiligen Schrift*, edited by Gaalyahu Cornfeld (Tel Aviv) and Johannes Botterweck (Bonn), Lübbe Verlag, 1969, Vol. 2, column 1238.

5. *Praktisches Bibellexicon*, Col. 854.

6. Acts 9:1–6.

7. Acts 9:18, 19.

8. Acts 24:5. In the original Greek text J. is also described as a "Nazarene" in Acts 2:28; 3:6; 4:10; 6:14; 22:8, 26. Although the grammatical form "Jesus the Nazarean" is unequivocal, the revised Lutheran edition of 1964 translates the same passage in the text as "Jesus of Nazareth." The so-called *Jerusalem Bible* correctly translates "Jesus, the Nazarean."

   The Nazareans were an ascetic branch of Jewish Christtianity that is also known under the concept of Ebionites and probably had a gospel related to Matthew's that originated in Syria.

   The translation of the revised Lutheran edition, as well as other translations such as the *New English Bible* of 1961, simply have the effect of strengthening the faith (cf. Raschke, Ch. 10).

9. Philippians 3:4–5.

10. Philippians 3:9.

11. The only biographical details of Jesus given by Paul are:

    a) Jesus was a Jew, "made of a woman, made under the law" (!) (Galatians 3:16; 4:4).

    b) He was descended from David (Romans 1:3).

    c) He preached only to Israel (!) "to confirm the promises made unto the fathers" (Romans 15:8).

    d) He was obedient to God even unto the death of the cross (Philippians 2:8).

    e) He appointed apostles (Galatians 1:17, 19).

f) He was reviled and crucified (Romans 15:3; 1 Corinthians 15:3; Galatians 2:19–20; 3:13).

g) His crucifixion was due to Jewish infamy (1 Thessalonians 2:15).

h) He rose again on the third day (1 Corinthians 15:4).

i) He appeared to Peter, the apostles, and the others, and, in a vision, to Paul (1 Corinthians 15:5–8).

k) He instituted the Last Supper (1 Corinthians 11:23).

l) And sits on the right hand of God (Romans 8:34).

(After Joel Carmichael, p. 44).

12. Heinz Zahrnt, *Es begann mit J. von Nazareth*, Kreuz Verlag, Stuttgart, 1960, p. 64.

CHAPTER TWELVE

1. Heinz Zahrnt, *Es begann mit J. von Nazareth—die Frage nach dem historischen J.*, Kreuz Verlag, Stuttgart, 1960, pp. 64, 65. (The Wrede quotations come from his book *Paul*, Religionsgeschichtliche Volksbücher I, 5, 6, Tübingen, 1904.)

2. William Wrede, *Paul*, quoted by W. G. Kümmel, *Das Neue Testament, Geschichte der Erforschung seiner Probleme.* Freiburg/Munich, 1958, pp. 377–82.

3. *Männer und Frauen des Neuen Testaments—Biblisches Taschenlexikon*, ed. by Friedrich Samuel Rothenberg, Verlag Brockhaus, 1966, p. 72.

4. Hugh J. Schonfield, *Unerhört, diese Christen—Geburt und Verwandlung der Urkirche*, Molden, 1969, p. 81.

5. *Die Bibel und ihre Welt—sine Enzyklopedie zur Heilegen Schrift*, ed. by Gaalyahu Cornfield (Tel Aviv) and Johannes Botterweck (Bonn), Lübbe Verlag, 1969, under Paul, Col. 1154.

6. Kurt Schubert, *Die Gemeinde vom Totan Meer—ihre Entstehung und ihre Lehren*, Reinhardt Verlag, Munich, 1958, pp. 134 and 135.

7. Mark 16:8 (verses 9–20 are a later addition).

8. Matthew 11:14; Matthew 17:12.

9. Mark 6:16.

10. Luke 14:13–31.

11. John 3.

12. Acts 15:22–29.

13. Albert Schweitzer, *The Mystique of the Apostle Paul*, Seabury, New York, 1954.

14. Carmichael, p. 216.

CHAPTER THIRTEEN

1. See *Inter alia* Exodus 24:6, 7; 1 Samuel 9:16; 1 Samuel 16.

2. Psalm 2:6, 7.

3. 2 Samuel 7:12, 14.

4. Psalm 89:21, 27, 28.

5. Exodus 4:22.

6. Jeremiah 31:7, 9.

7. Carmichael, p. 203-4.

8. Schonfield, p. 286.

9. Carmichael, p. 219.

CHAPTER FOURTEEN

1. Heinz Zahrnt, *Es begann mit Jesus von Nazareth*, Kreuz Verlag, 1960, p. 112.

2. An annotated bibliography on this subject can be found in Shalom Ben Chorin, *Jesus, Bruder J.—der Nazarener in jüdischer Sicht*, List Verlag, 1967.

3. Martin Luther, explanation of the second article of the Creed.

4. Ernst Fuchs in *Theolgie für Nichttheologen—ABC protestantischen Denkens*, ed. by H. J. Schultz, Kreuz Verlag, 1964, under J. Christ.

5. Karl Rahner in *Das Glaubensbekenntnis—Aspekte für ein neues Verständnis*, ed. by Gerhard Rein, Kreuz Verlag, p. 20.

6. Dietrich Bonhoeffer, *Wer ist und wer war Christus?—seine Geschichte und sein Geheimnis*, Furche Verlag, 1962, p. 60.

7. Ibid.

8. Ibid.

9. "Jesus" is the Greek form of the name Joshua, which was pronounced Jehoshua or Jeshua around the birth of Christ. Joshua means "Yahweh helps" and is explained as follows in Matthew 1:21: ". . . thou shalt call his name JESUS: for he shall save his people from their sins." At that time it was one of the common Jewish names.

BIBLIOGRAPHY

OLD TESTAMENT

COOLS, P. J., editor, German edition: Theodor Schegler, OSB, *Geschichte und Religion des Alten Testaments*, Walter, Olten, 1965.

CORNFELD, GAALYAHU (Tel Aviv), and BOTTERWECK, G. JOHANNES (Bonn), editors, *Die Bibel und ihre Welt— Eine Enzyklopädie zur Heiligen Schrift*, 2 vols., Gustav Lübbe Verlag, 1969.

EICHROTH, WALTER, *Religionsgeschichte Israels*, Prancke Verlag, Berne and Munich, 1969.

MAYER, REINHOLD, *Der Babylonische Talmud*, selected and translated by Reinhold Mayer, Goldmann Verlag, Munich, 1965.

QUMRAN AND THE ESSENES

ALLEGRO, JOHN M., *The Dead Sea Scrolls*—Penguin, 1956.

BRAUN, HERBERT, *Qumran und das Neue Testament*, 2 vols., C. B. Mohr, Tübingen, 1969.

BURROWS, MILLAR, *More Light on the Dead Sea Scrolls*, Viking, New York, 1958.

CROSS, FRANK MOORE, JR., *The Ancient Library of Qumran and Modern Biblical Studies*, Anchor Books, New York, 1961.

DANIELOU, JEAN, *Qumran und der Urserung des Christentums*, Matthias Grünewald Verlag, Mainz, 1959.

173

FLAVIUS JOSEPHUS, *History of the Jewish War*, translated by G. A. Williamson, Penguin Classics, 1970.

FLUSSER, DAVID, *Qumran und die Zwölf*, Leiden, 1965.

GASTER, THEODORE H., *The Dead Sea Scriptures* in English translation with introduction and notes, Doubleday, New York, 1956.

SCHUBERT, KURT, *The Dead Sea Community: Its Origins and Its Teachings*, Humanities, 1958.

WILSON, EDMUND, *The Scrolls from the Dead Sea*, Oxford University Press, 1955.

YADIN, YIGAEL, *Masada—Der letzte Kampf um die Festung des Herodes*, Hoffmann and Campe, Hamburg, 1967.

JESUS AND HIS AGE

DANIEL-ROPS, HENRI, *Jesus and His Times*, Dutton, New York, 1954.

MAERTENS, THIERRY, *Heidnisch-jüdische Wurzeln der christlichen Feste*, Matthias Grünewald Verlag, Mainz, 1965.

ROTHENBERG, FRIEDRICH SAMUEL, *Männer und Frauen des Neuen Testaments*, Brockhaus, Wuppertal, 1966.

SCHULTZ, HANS JURGEN, editor, *Die Zeit Jesu—Kontexte*, Kreuz Verlag, Stuttgart, 1966.

JESUS AND HIS LIFE

BEN CHORIN, SHALOM, *Jesus—Bruder Jesus—Der Nazarener in jüdischer Sicht*, List Verlag, Munich, 1967.

BONHOEFFER, DIETRICH, *Wer ist und wer war Jesus Christus —Seine Geschichte und sein Geheimnis*, Furche Verlag, Hamburg, 1962.

BRAUN, HERBERT, *Jesus—Der Mann aus Nazareth und seine Zeit*, Kreuz Verlag, Stuttgart, 1969.

BULTMANN, RUDOLF, *Jesus*, C. B. Mohr, Tübingen, 1926; Siebenstern Taschenbuch, Munich, 1965 (2d edition).

CARMICHAEL, JOEL, *The Death of Jesus*, Macmillan, New York, 1962.

DESCHNER, KARLHEINZ, *Jesusbilder in theologischer Sicht*, List Verlag, Munich, 1966.

FLUSSER, DAVID, *Jesus*, Rowohlt Monographie, 1968.

SCHULTZ, HANS JÜRGEN, editor, *Theologie für Nichttheologen—ABC protestantischen Denkens*, Kreuz Verlag, 1964.

———, *Die Wahrheit der Ketzer*, Kreuz Verlag, Stuttgart, 1968.

STAUFFER, ETHELBERT, *Jesus — Gestalt und Geschichte*, Francke Verlag, Berne, Dalp Taschenbuch, 1957.

ZAHRNT, HEINZ, *Es begann mit Jesus von Nazareth—Die Frage nach dem historischen Jesus*, Kreuz Verlag, Stuttgart, 1960.

THE ORIGIN OF CHRISTIANITY

BEN CHORIN, SHALOM, *Paulus—Der Völkerapostel in jüdischer Sicht*, List Verlag, Munich, 1970.

REIN, GERHARD, editor, *Das Glaubensbekenntnis—Aspekte für ein neues Verständnis*, Kreuz Verlag, Stuttgart, 1967.

SCHONFIELD, HUGH J., *The Passover Plot*, Geis, New York, 1966.

———, *The Secrets of the Dead Sea Scrolls*, Peter Smith, New York, 1957.

SCHWEITZER, ALBERT, *The Mysticism of Paul the Apostle*, Seabury, New York, 1954.

WESTERMANN, CLAUS, editor, *Theologie, VI u. 12 Hauptbegriffe*, Kreuz Verlag, Stuttgart, 1967.

ISAAC, JULES, *Genesis des Antisemitismus ver und nach Christus:* Europa Verlag, Vienna, 1969.

RENGSTROF, HEINRICH, and KORTZFLEISCH, SIEGFRIED, editors, *Kirche und Synagoge—Handbuch zur Geschichte ven Christen und Juden,* Verlag, Stuttgart, 1968.

SCHULTZ, HANS JÜRGEN, *Juden—Christen—Deutsche,* Kreuz Verlag, Stuttgart, 1961.